SHAMBA SHENANIGANS

ABOUT THE AUTHOR

JOHN MUIGAI MUCAI HAS A PH.D. in Business Administration from the University of Nairobi. He is a Certified Public Accountant of Kenya too. He is an alumnus of the United States International University, where he graduated with an MSc in Management and Organizational Development and a BSc cum laude in Information Systems & Technology. He retired from Coca-Cola East & Central Africa Ltd in 2017 and has since been pursuing various hobbies and entrepreneurial interests.

JOHN'S WIFE, SUSAN MUMBI MUIGAI, is a crucial player in most of the stories narrated in the book. She is a businesswoman. She loves gardening and has an avid passion for cooking. She, too, is currently pursuing various hobbies and entrepreneurial interests.

SHAMBA SHENANIGANS

A Collection of Riveting True Stories

John Mucai

with the invaluable support of
Susan Mumbi Muigai

Copyright © 2020 by John Mucai

All rights reserved. No part of this publication may be reproduced, stored, or transmitted in any form or by any means, electronic, mechanical, photocopying, recording, scanning, or otherwise, without written permission from the publisher. It is illegal to copy this book, post it to a website, or distribute it by any other means without permission.

John Mucai asserts the moral right to be identified as the author of this work.

John Mucai has no responsibility for the persistence or accuracy of URLs for external or third-party Internet Websites referred to in this publication and does not guarantee that any content on such Websites is, or will remain, accurate or appropriate.

Designations used by companies to distinguish their products are often claimed as trademarks. All brand names and product names used in this book and on its cover are trade names, service marks, trademarks, and registered trademarks of their respective owners. The publishers and the book are not associated with any product or vendor mentioned in this book. None of the companies referenced within the book have
endorsed the book.

For any further information, contact John Muigai Mucai at the following address:
P.O. Box 2069 - 00606, Nairobi, Kenya. Email:
johnmucai@gmail.com

Cover design by Linda Matama

ISBN 978-9966-139-07-8

To our son Allan and our daughter Anne, the primary source of inspiration and encouragement for the MUCAI Quick Read series.

"Variety's the very spice of life, that gives it all its flavor."

WILLIAM COWPER

CONTENTS

Foreword xi
Preface xiii
Acknowledgments xv
Chapter 1: A Tale of Urban Mischief 1
Chapter 2: Small Gesture, Big Impact 15
Chapter 3: Drama in the Savanna................................. 21
Chapter 4: Challenges of a Promising Potato Enterprise   35
Chapter 5: Hay and Debris 47
Chapter 6: Charcoal Burning Venture Beats Cash Crops   63
Chapter 7: Physics 101: Mini-Irrigation Project............. 75
Chapter 8: The KPLC Song 89
Chapter 9: The Largest Market for Avocados is China ... 105
Chapter 10: The Land Where Monday Never Comes 115
Chapter 11: You can get Chapatis at the Lands Office ... 123
Chapter 12: Second Tale of Urban Mischief 133
Chapter 13: The Tent of Gastronomical Delights............. 143
Epilogue 157
Selected Photographs 163
Translations 169
References 171
Other Books by John Mucai.................................... 175
Index 181

FOREWORD

SHAMBA SHENANIGANS IS THE FIRST in the MUCAI Quick Read series. The books in the series are for the reader who has a few hours on their hands that they could use to indulge in light and educative entertainment. For example, a passenger on a bus, train, cruise ship, or plane heading to a distant destination, a tourist relaxing on a beach on the beautiful coast of Mombasa, or someone just relaxing at home after a long day at work.

The books in the series cover a broad spectrum of topics to titillate the reader's intellect:
- humorous biographical stories
- accounts of captivating historical events
- narratives of extraordinary science
- journeys towards spiritual enlightenment
- intrigues in business
- strategy, and
- thought-provoking philosophical ideas

The objective of the series is to encourage the reader to think about the world differently and positively.

PREFACE

MY WIFE, SUSAN, AND I enjoy spending time outdoors, preferably up-country - this is our biggest hobby. Over time, we have realized that we can pursue the hobby by engaging in various value-adding activities. The consequence of this is that we have often found ourselves entangled in different types of exciting shenanigans. We have learned useful life lessons in each instance. We believe that others can learn from these experiences too. This book shares these experiences and a few others that occurred in other settings.

One important lesson we have learned is that it is always better to look on the bright side of things, even in the most unpleasant situations. Life is far too short and far too precious. Accordingly, we share the experiences with a light touch and tongue-in-cheek in instances where this makes good sense.

You will find some stories hilarious, others complex, and others mundane. The idea is to evoke a broad spectrum of emotions to optimize your reading experience. For example, if you feel a little down because of a small indignity done to you by some people, then "The Tent of Gastronomical Delights" will lift your spirits. If there is a little villain in you that is nudging to come out, then "Drama in the Savanna" will help you stretch your imagination in a fun way. If someone has done a great deed and you wish to encourage them, then "Small Gesture, Big Impact" may motivate you to take action. A common thread across all the stories is that each experience contains one or more valuable life lessons.

Some experiences are yet to run their full course. They are playing out even as this book goes to press. The new life lessons from these experiences will be included in another book in the series or a new edition of this book.

The names of the characters in the book are real, except in a few instances where fictitious names were more appropriate to avoid any unintended anxiety or embarrassment to the actual persons. Enjoy!

ACKNOWLEDGMENTS

THE ALMIGHTY GOD HAS BEEN the shining guiding light throughout my life, even in this book project. I will always remain steadfastly thankful to Him.

This book project would not have been possible without the immense support of my wife, Susan, one of the key characters in the book. She reviewed the manuscript multiple times and helped clarify several events that happened many years ago. My son Allan and my daughter Anne also provided invaluable assistance in reviewing the book. I owe Susan, Allan, and Anne a significant debt of gratitude.

I would also like to thank Rose Muyah, Fred Mucai, and Nzisa Kattambo for their invaluable contributions in editing the book.

CHAPTER 1

A Tale of Urban Mischief

> *"Life is like riding a bicycle. To keep
> your balance, you must keep moving."*
> —Albert Einstein

AN UNFORGETTABLE INCIDENT OF UNBLUSHING deception that occurred in the 1980s is the main inspiration for this story. It happened bizarrely and is therefore narrated as a monster tale. It is similar to the monster tales our aunties and grandmothers told us when we were kids. There are interesting lessons to be learned from the story.

◆◆◆

THERE IS AN INCIDENT OF DECEPTION that occurred in the 1980s that reminds me of my childhood days when stories told by our grandparents or aunts instilled enormous fear in us. I have never understood why our aunties and grandparents did this. Perhaps it was to teach us a sense of caution in our future dealings with other mortals, many of whom are prone to deception, as I was to learn later in my adult life.

I spent the better part of my childhood in Nakuru, my birthplace. I have very fond memories of the place. When I was growing up there, it was said to be the cleanest town in Kenya. I can still see in my distant memory the beautiful, green, and well-manicured ground in front of the Nakuru Railway Station.

I also remember vividly the open spaces and the green grounds on which my friends and I played different types of games. The games included football, banta, tiara, climbing trees, skidding (on the muddy field during the rainy season), and bird hunting around Lake Nakuru.

There was a motorcar racing track at Langalanga, near Lake Nakuru. Our parents would occasionally take us there during weekends to watch many beautifully colored cars or motorcycles competing against each other.

The most enjoyable pastime of all was joining the Luhya *isukuti* dancers and wildly gyrating our hips, legs, and elbows to the *isukuti* drumbeats as the dance troupe passed by our home. The *isukuti* dancers wore multicolored skirts made of sisal. Some of the men wore black and white feather hats too. The men danced bare-chested, while the women wore loose vests and different types of head scuffs. It was amazing to watch them dance. Most of all, it was free entertainment. It used to happen only once in a while, and we could hardly get enough of it.

The *isukuti* dance troupe would commence their journey several miles away at Shabab. They would then make their way through various estates in town. We could hear the *isukuti* drumbeats, the metal rattles, and the accompanying blowing of the horn from far as the dance troupe approached our estate. We went into a frenzy as we waited for our turn to join them.

Men, women, boys, and girls of all ages would join the troupe and dance vigorously to their hearts' content. They would then gradually exit from the party for others to join in as the *isukuti* journey continued to the next estate. The final destination was at Kivumbini, the southernmost part of Nakuru at the time, at sundown. It was an immensely fulfilling experience. I am sometimes overcome by nostalgia when I reminisce about this awesome *isukuti* dance.

My parents must have seen through this perpetual enjoyment and were keen to ensure their children did not grow into narrow-minded urbanized individuals. In other words, individuals who could not speak their mother tongue or who could not clearly distinguish between right and wrong. Or worse still, individuals who would live under the illusion that chips and sausages grew on trees. Accordingly, they made sure that we spent a good chunk of our school holidays at Matathia with our cousins, aunts, and grandparents, during which we would learn about our culture and other aspects of life.

Matathia is in the Uplands region of central Kenya. Average temperatures there can sometimes go down to 8 degrees Celsius during the cold season, compared to 12 degrees Celsius for Nakuru. There are also times when it becomes foggy for a good part of the day.

My brothers and I didn't particularly look forward to going there. From our perspective, it was always colder than the South Pole. We also had to milk cows early in the morning when our friends in Nakuru were still in bed. Not only that. After milking the cows, we had to take the milk to the dairy at Kimende shopping center, about three kilometers away. The journey to the dairy included climbing some very steep ground behind my grandparents' house. The climb took about five minutes, but it felt like one hour. I remember one time when my cousin Muthee and I were taking milk to the dairy. I accidentally skidded and went tumbling down like a ball, along with my can containing about 5 liters of milk. It was an ugly incident, but such events were considered normal. There was no such thing as First Aid, so I just had to let the minor bruises I had sustained heal naturally.

My brothers and I also found it a bit tough to cope with the pure and refined local language spoken by other children in Matathia. It made us feel uncomfortable when communicating with other kids. It took several holidays to speak the local language fluently, confidently, and without an urban accent. On a slightly positive note, though, we cheekily frowned upon those kids who had challenges pronouncing certain words when it came to Kiswahili and English. For example, they would pronounce the letter "l" as "r" and vice versa. The term "rural" was "*lulal*," and "lorry" was "*rolly*."

SHAMBA SHENANIGANS

The difficulty in pronouncing the word lorry seemed a little peculiar. The kids could correctly pronounce the letters "r" and "l" but seemed to switch them around involuntarily. At times we would just burst into uncontrollable laughter.

Our times in Matathia were a kaleidoscope of enriching experiences that evoked different fulfilling and memorable emotions.

One of my most vivid memories is the story-time around a fireplace in my aunt's kitchen in the evenings. The kitchen was a small mud hut with a grass-thatched roof. There was a fireplace in the middle consisting of three stones arranged in a triangular shape. There was a simple structure above the fireplace that served dual purposes. Firstly, as a temporary storage area for kindling. Secondly, as a drier for wet firewood. The structure was called *itara*.

In the late afternoon, the girls would go to the forest to collect firewood and fetch water from a nearby stream. On the other hand, the boys would be involved in other activities, such as livestock herding. Later in the evening, we would all sit around the fireplace and watch as our aunt, Tata Mweru, cooked supper.

Most of the time, the meal would be *githeri*, a nutritious mixture of maize and beans. Occasionally, potatoes and green pumpkin leaves would be added, and the mixture pounded to form a delicious paste, *mukimo*. The recipe for the typical dish was easy to remember:

In the early afternoon, pour four pints of water into a clay pot. Boil the water until it becomes dangerously hot. Add one teaspoon of salt. Stir for two seconds. Pour in three bowls of beans. Wait for three minutes. Add an equal measure of maize. Leave to simmer for about four hours. Later in the evening, add some potatoes and green pumpkin leaves. Spend the next one-hour storytelling, preferably stories of monsters, so that the six or so pair of beaming eyes do not go to sleep before the meal is ready. Take a spoonful of the food from the pot, and taste it. If well-cooked, remove the pot from the fire and pound its contents with a muiko to form a thick and smooth paste. Now proceed to serve the food to the hungry innocent young souls gathered around the fireplace. Continue telling stories or riddles until the children start falling asleep one by one. Have the small ones carried to bed, including those pretending to be asleep but forgot to wash their feet with cold water, as is mandatory every evening.

The stories about monsters were exceptionally frightening, but I loved them. They sounded so real that even the wind's slight whirling as Tata Mweru narrated them sent chills down our spines. The blowing of the wind created a perfect illusion that a monster was just about to attack. Additionally, the wind's sporadic whistling sound would provide a natural sound effect that would amplify the fear-factor ten times. There was no way any of us would walk alone the 20 feet from the hut to the main house for fear of being accosted by a monster.

There were times when the shock value of the stories would be so intense that later in the evening, some children could not even dare step out of bed to relieve themselves. The ones who had weak bladders answered the call of nature right there, in bed. Suffering the humiliation of your wet blankets being dried in the sun, publicly for everyone to see, was better than risking the possibility of being swallowed up alive by *irimu ria nyakondo*, the monster, or getting clobbered by the other vicious monster *mutheca itu*, on your way to the john.

As you read the monster tale that follows, picture yourself in a small hut, in the company of other children, around a fireplace, listening to aunt Mweru.

> *Once upon a time, in the 1980s, there lived monsters in the concrete jungle of Nairobi. Small monsters lived in Kirinyaga Road's bushes and fed on ignorant migrants from the rural areas. Other monsters were medium in size but a little more sophisticated and fed on other little monsters or even medium monsters. Then there were the huge monsters. These lived in impressive quarters, mostly in high-rise concrete structures, and swallowed up everything that came their way.*
>
> *One day, one of the small mischievous monsters, disguised as a human being, visited a young*

couple called John and Susan. The monster said that his name was Njoroge.

Neither Susan nor John had ever met or even heard of this person in their entire lives. Still, he introduced himself as a close relative who had known them for many years. Njoroge introduced himself as follows:

"Do you remember Kabuthi, the great grandfather of Wacera? Wacera who lived in Githunguri with Wacuka. Now, Wacuka was the sister of Kabuthi and the third wife of my grandfather Njoroge. Njoroge moved to Njoro after the declaration of emergency, just before independence. I lived with him as a kid until I reached adolescence, when I moved to Kimende to join secondary school. It was while at Kimende that I became acquainted with your cousins in Matathia. How are they now? It has been a while since I spoke to them."

John and Susan recanted their experience of meeting Njoroge as follows:

"When he finished introducing himself, Susan and I were so confused and overwhelmed with the genealogical intricacies of the extended family that it was even embarrassing to seek any clarification. We just nodded occasionally to

signify our wholesome understanding of the genealogy. Indeed, we had no choice but to succumb to welcoming this unique visitor with open arms naively.

"He turned out to be a real chatterbox. The afternoon that he spent in our house expired almost in a flash.

"He revisited us a week later, on a Sunday. We accorded him the same generous reception. The chattering was the same as before. As he was departing, he asked us to lend him KShs 100/=, which we did happily.

"Njoroge showed up again on the third Sunday. We had become such wonderful relatives. The Sunday visits had become a standard routine. After the usual chattering, he borrowed an additional KShs 200/= for repayment in a few days, without fail, so he said.

"By now, the constant visits were beginning to wear us down. Njoroge had become a serial visitor and a serial borrower, but we tolerated it. After several more Sunday visits, it became unbearable.
"He was not welcome anymore, but we were too nice to show it.

SHAMBA SHENANIGANS

"On one particular Sunday, what was to become his penultimate Sunday visit, he came on a bicycle. As he was leaving, he requested us to store the bike for him for collection in a few days. This request seemed very strange. Why would someone want us to store a bicycle for him? Could he not store it in his own house? We started feeling a bit jittery about the source of the bike and politely declined the request.

"But before leaving, he asked for yet another small loan of KShs 300/=. We lent him the money. He swore to repay all the money borrowed from us by the following Sunday, "come what may!" so he said.

"In the next two days, through some extraordinary luck, I, John, discovered a scheme that would ensure that Njoroge would never ever borrow any more money from us. It was a simple and straightforward scheme that I discovered by sheer coincidence while having a casual conversation with my workmate Kiama.

"Kiama told me that his friends had set up an informal money-lending business. The interest rate that they charged was high. But their unique value proposition was that a borrower could get a loan in minutes if they met all the loan conditions.

SHAMBA SHENANIGANS

"Kiama did not mention how the money lenders enforced repayment of the money, but I was not too keen on the details. I suspected that the money lenders used unconventional methods that always worked, even with trick stars such as Njoroge.

"One unique feature of the loans was that the outstanding balance quickly ballooned if the loan installments were not paid by the due date. I later learned that delays in repayment were surreptitiously encouraged by the money lenders. This type of loan was the perfect banking product for Njoroge.

"The following Sunday was to become Njoroge's final visit to our house. Rather than lend him the KShs 400/= that he requested, I happily handed him a handwritten note addressed to Kiama. In the note, I asked Kiama to use his best influence to ensure that the money lenders gave Njoroge a loan quickly and on the best terms possible.

"After handing Njoroge the note, I assured him that Kiama was a trusted work colleague. Further, I had no doubt that Kiama would go out of his way to ensure that Njoroge received the KShs 400/= loan.

SHAMBA SHENANIGANS

"That afternoon, as I parted ways with Njoroge, a certain feeling of well-being flowed through my veins. We had finally contrived a scheme that would quickly and effectively halt Njoroge's constant borrowing of money, money that he had no intention of repaying. He would no longer have an excuse to solicit cash from Susan, me, or any other person.

"Two days later, I received a call from Kiama, who was then working at the head office in the Central Business District of Nairobi. I worked at my employer's factory in the industrial area at the time. Still, I continued to enjoy a close professional working relationship with Kiama. On this particular day, Kiama seemed to be in exceptionally high spirits. And why not? He had performed a deed on my behalf that he believed would make me extremely happy, further solidifying our friendship.

"He triumphantly announced that upon receiving my note from my relative, Njoroge, he had tried his best to give the relative utmost assistance. He had contacted the moneylenders to ensure that Njoroge was given a loan without any delay whatsoever. And indeed, the loan process had gone very smoothly. The moneylenders had already disbursed KShs 4,000/= to Njoroge. The transaction had been completed about 30 minutes before Kiama called me. Further, Kiama had signed the loan application form on my behalf as the guarantor of the loan. However, I still needed to sign the forms, at my convenience, for the sake of good order.

"My heart skipped several beats! "Has he already taken the money?" I inquired. "Yes. These moneylenders are very efficient. They do not waste any time."

"I felt a mixture of anger, outrage, helplessness, and betrayal of the highest order. I had just lost a clean KShs 4,000/= to a conman while trying to avoid giving him a loan ten times less.

"I never saw or heard from Njoroge ever again. I had inadvertently become a guarantor of KShs 4,000/= lent to the king of conmen himself.

"I repaid the full amount, including the extortionate interest, in several excruciatingly painful installments. My only respite was the knowledge that, by that act of deceit, Njoroge had undoubtedly earned himself a nice hot spot somewhere in the underworld."

SHAMBA SHENANIGANS

So, children. When you grow up and go into the big urban jungles, be careful of the small mischievous monsters. They can devour you and quickly disappear into the urban forest without a trace.

This monster story never ceases to frighten even the very bold ones. A key lesson from it is that sometimes it is better to say "no," rather than seek less painful but convoluted ways of trying to accommodate others.

CHAPTER 2

Small Gesture, Big Impact

*"Be the change that you wish to see in
the world."*
—Mahatma Gandhi

SUSAN, OUTRAGED BY THE RAPID loss of greenery in Nairobi, made a small but unique personal gesture in 2005 that may have set in motion a positive sentiment within the local government system. Susan's simple action may have helped accelerate a significant environmental conservation initiative in Nairobi, benefiting hundreds of thousands of Nairobi residents.

◆◆◆

WE LOVE TREES, PERHAPS, a bug that we caught from the great environmentalist and Nobel laureate, the late Professor Wangari Mathai. We have planted countless trees during the past few years. The pleasure of observing trees grow from little seedlings into mature, woody, and leafy plants that provide forest cover, a habitat for birds, and protection from soil erosion and other means of human sustenance is hard to put in words. During the rainy season, we seek out and take full advantage of any opportunities for planting trees. In 2005, engrossed with concern about the rate at which the trees in Nairobi were disappearing, Susan noticed something positive that was happening at Kangemi. She decided to perform a small gesture that she hoped would boost the initiative to accelerate the environmental conservation efforts. She wrote a letter to the Standard newspaper expressing her desire to donate 500 assorted tree seedlings for planting along the Kangemi to Kabete dual carriageway. The Standard paper highlighted the matter in "The Standard Interactive" section (Waiyaki, 2005). The report read as follows:

> *For a long time, Kangemi has been an awful and unpleasant center due to massive garbage dumping all over, writes a resident, Susan Muigai. It was dusty, smelly, muddy, smoky, risky, and noisy.*
>
> *But there has been a tremendous improvement. The place is now greener with no garbage or the awful smell. It now looks quite peaceful and orderly. The next move, which would have an even bigger impact on the environment and beauty of Kangemi, is to plant trees along the road from Kianda College all the way to where Kabete police*

station is located, she suggests. And Susan says she would like to donate 500 trees (jacaranda, casuarina) during the rainy season. John Gakuo, do you want to accept this gift?

Responding to the press report, John Gakuo, the then Town Clerk of the Nairobi City Council, wrote a piece in the "Right of Reply" section of "Face the Facts" in The Standard newspaper (Gakuo, 2005):

> I refer to an article appearing on 6th April 2005 in the Standard under the heading "Women's Donation to Kangemi."
>
> I wish to express my most candid gratitude for Susan Muigai's appreciation of what the City Council is doing to conserve the environment at Kangemi, which was hitherto in a stinking mess.
>
> I also deeply appreciate her willingness to join hands with the council in making Kangemi an even better place to live in.
>
> Her pledge to donate 500 trees (Jacaranda and Casuarina) to the council for planting along the dual carriageway at Kangemi could not have come at a better time. The council is already in the process of massive preparation of the ground to plant trees at Kangemi stretching right from the

Kabete Police Station bridge to past Nairobi School at Kari. This will constitute phase I. The second phase at a later stage will commence from Nyayo Stadium roundabout to the junction of Jomo Kenyatta International Airport. I would appreciate it if part of Susan Muigai's donation could be Nandi Flame. However, should she not be in a position to donate Nandi Flame, Susan's goodwill gesture will still be crucial assistance as we need these trees for planting along the dual carriageway between Ruaraka and Muthaiga Police Station.

For further details, could Susan very kindly get in touch with my Director of Environment at City Hall.

John Gakuo, Town Clerk
___

Responding to Gakuo's letter, Susan reached out to the Environment Department at City Hall. The officer-in-charge invited her to what was supposed to be an elaborate public ceremony during which the Council would officially receive the donation. However, Susan was not ready for the media spotlight. She suggested a lower-key event. The Council organized the event where Susan donated several jacarandas, casuarina, and flame trees. She was immensely grateful for the positive reaction that her gesture had received from City Hall.

SHAMBA SHENANIGANS

The City Council started planting trees along the dual carriageway a few days later. We will never know whether Susan's simple action was the trigger for that activity or whether it was just a matter of pure coincidence. However, from Susan's perspective, something was, at long last, being done to improve the environment, and her donation of Nandi flames and other assorted trees would was an important contribution towards that effort.

Within four years, the dual carriageway had become an indelible mark of beauty in Nairobi. There was pleasant greenery on both sides of the highway.

The other ending to this story is that all these beautiful trees, including Susan's Nandi flames, were cut down in 2018 to pave the way for an expansion of the highway. However, the critical point is that Susan's small but unique gesture made a difference in beautifying a small part of Nairobi that hundreds of thousands of Nairobi residents enjoyed for more than ten years. So, why hold back on executing those small noble deeds you have in mind?

CHAPTER 3

Drama in the Savanna

> "In three words I can sum up everything I've learned about life: it goes on."
> —Robert Frost

OUR LOVE OF TREES LED us on a tree planting escapade in the savanna grassland of Longonot. However, the occasional wanton destruction of the young trees by herdsmen looking for green pasture for their livestock disrupted this undertaking. The herdsmen's impunity eventually turned into an exciting game of hide-and-seek between goats and their herdsmen and a spy who hails from the grasslands of Longonot aided by a team of astute savanna vigilantes. The result was the capture of the prime perpetrators of the destruction, but who ended up going scot-free in an equally dramatic fashion and at a small expense on our part, to boot.

SHAMBA SHENANIGANS

◆◆◆

OUR QUEST TO ENHANCE THE greenery in the countryside, even if only in a small way, mutated into periodic visits to Longonot, within the Rift Valley, southeast of Lake Naivasha.

Longonot is about 15 kilometers from Naivasha town via the Old Naivasha Road (C88). Most of the land there is savanna grassland, with bush and shrubs in areas that have not been interfered with by human activity. The soils are predominantly volcanic and contain a large percentage of silica and oxygen (Girma, Rossiter, Hennemann, & G.r., 1970). The average annual rainfall is 27 inches (677mm) annually, while the average yearly temperature is 17 degrees Celsius (Climare-Data.org., 2019). There are times when it gets quite windy too. It is a pleasant place to live, but because of the extended periods of warm, dry weather during the year, rain-fed production of food crops is a challenge. Accordingly, most of the land lies idle.

Many years ago, the land belonged to colonial settlers who used it primarily for large-scale cattle ranching. Subsequently, land buying companies acquired the land and subdivided it into multiple small plots. Most of the parcels were not marked. Therefore, it was usually a free-for-all for the local herdsmen, especially during the dry season when they struggled to find pasture for their cattle, goats, and sheep.

Several years ago, land in this area was going for low prices. We acquired a few acres and decided to plant trees on an experimental basis. We started by planting 500 acacia (acacia *xanthophoea*), 500 eucalypti, and 400 *mukima* (*grevillea robusta*) trees. We planted 100 other trees of different types. Susan also donated different varieties of trees to a local primary school, Kamuyu Primary School, with the expectation that in a few years, the trees would create a pleasant aesthetic look for the school and shade and fresh air that would benefit the school children.

A fully-grown acacia tree has a flat top and a yellow trunk. It is indigenous and is common near Lake Naivasha and Lake Nakuru. It is also widely known as the fever tree. Apart from its beauty, it has multiple uses. For example, use as food for giraffes and as firewood for cooking. It is also used by local artisans to make carvings. The vast majority of the acacia trees we planted survived and thrived well, even during the hot, dry periods. The eucalyptus tree, also called blue gum, is not indigenous to Naivasha or Kenya. Its origins are in Australia. It has become a common feature in Kenya's urban and rural areas. It grows pretty quickly relative to other trees. Some species can reach a height of up to 100 meters.

In recent years many farmers have been growing eucalyptus trees for sale to the Kenya Power & Lighting Company for electricity poles. The trees have various other purposes, such as firewood for cooking and timber for building houses. Their main disadvantage is that they drain the soil quite rapidly. Because of this, they can adversely affect other crops near them (Karmal, 1993). Accordingly, we planted them in a separate portion of the shamba, where they would not adversely affect other plants.

The eucalyptus trees grew well in the first three years, but some started wilting in the third year. We learned that the reason for the wilting was that the roots had reached a depth containing porous pumice rocks. The few trees that survived grew very slowly, but we were doubtful about their prospects for long-term survival.

Ironically, pumice is mined by some locals and sold to large-scale flower farms for use in hydroponic flower production. The many man-made craters in some parts of the Longonot grassland are the direct result of this mining activity.

The *mukima* tree is also known as the Australian silver oak. It is widespread in Kenya's coffee-growing central highlands, including Kiambu, Embu, Meru, and Kirinyaga. The tree was introduced in Kenya from Australia for use as shade for coffee trees. It grows quite fast relative to other trees, reaching a height of 20 meters when mature. It has multiple applications too. It can be used as timber, firewood, and even for soil conservation. Many farmers also use it as a windbreaker.

We were keen to see how the *mukima* trees would perform in the dry savanna grassland. To our complete amazement, the trees grew very well. We had planted them along two edges of a rectangular-shaped piece of land, and after three years, they formed a very nice-looking hedge. We left them to grow freely. They have since become excellent windbreakers. The trees' slight tilt away from the windward direction has become an exciting aesthetic feature that is nice to watch, particularly on windy days.

The multiple varieties of other trees that we planted did not do well. We had planted them randomly for curiosity to see how they would do in the Longonot area.

We always looked forward to weekends when we would travel to Longonot to check on the trees, including the ones Susan had donated to Kamuyu Primary School. During the rainy season, we would re-plant the ones that had succumbed to the dry climatic conditions. The replacements would be the species we had discovered had the best chances of survival based on our first-hand knowledge of the trees we had planted before.

◆◆◆

However, whenever something good happens, Beelzebub is always lurking around the corner to spoil the party. We started receiving reports from neighbors that herdsmen had, from time to time, trespassed onto our land, searching for green pastures for their livestock. In the process, they had damaged some trees. This information was quite upsetting. Through the help of Mwangi, our local confidant, we sought assistance from the local Chief.

The Chief was very helpful. He issued a stern warning to the herdsmen. This communication seemed to have worked well because the herdsmen stopped trespassing on the land for a while.

We were determined to continue planting as many trees as possible, including replacing those damaged by livestock. Accordingly, we organized a massive tree planting exercise during one memorable rainy season. The initiative required the collective effort of about 30 people from the neighborhood. It was quite a sight to behold as the work was going on.

Several weeks later, as the young trees began to take root, the herdsmen decided it was Christmas time for their goats. They cut the wire fence on one side of the shamba and herded their goats into the shamba.

The damage caused by the goats was devilishly infuriating. We did not know what to do or even where to start in dealing with the problem. The herdsmen persisted in the illegal activity, on and off, for several months.

Sometime in early 2016, we reached out to some neighbors for advice on how to deal with the issue and resolve it permanently. We learned that the only effective way of dealing with the miscreants was to report them to the Anti-Stock Theft Unit soldiers, whose base was about five kilometers from the shamba. We followed the advice and reported the matter.

And indeed, the Anti-Stock Theft Unit soldiers were willing to help. There was only one catch: they could only take action if we provided physical evidence linking the damaged trees to specific herdsmen. This policy made much sense, but how could one obtain physical evidence for this kind of infraction? Showing the damaged trees to the soldiers was not good enough. One had to demonstrate the link between damaged trees and specific herdsmen. The herdsmen were probably aware of this requirement, which is perhaps why they trespassed into the property with impunity.

The difficulty of the challenge notwithstanding, we would not throw up our hands in despair. There had to be a way of dealing with the problem. We thought hard about it and concluded that the only way to get the required evidence was to set a trap for the herdsmen. We needed to catch them red-handed. The scheme would necessitate hiring a spy to watch over the land, who would promptly alert the Anti-Stock Theft Unit soldiers when the herdsmen trespassed into the property. This plan was excellent but was an equally daunting mission. We decided to execute it anyway.

We were so furious about the wanton destruction of the trees that if we had the ability, we would have sought the services of James Bond himself to catch the miscreants and their bleating sheep. And if James Bond was on another mission, then we would have hired Sherlock Holmes, who could "eliminate the impossible, and whatever remained, however improbable, would have been the truth" (Fields, Javier, & Doyle, 2012), the verifiable truth that the Anti-Stock Theft Unit soldiers needed.

It turned out that we did not need to go very far to get a good spy. Mwangi Kiiru, a neighboring farmer and a close confidant, volunteered to do the job. The image of a Martini-swigging James Bond character with a license to kill probably comes to the reader's mind. But that was not it. Firstly, we did not want anyone or any animal to die. Secondly, the villains were not in the Goldfinger league. They were just free spirits that roamed the open savanna grassland, adorned in a simple blanket or *shuka*, without any other clothing to protect their vital organs from the elements. Most of them carried rudimentary weapons, such as a *rungu*, a *njora*, or both, for personal protection. If, perchance, you found them grazing their livestock on your property and asked them why they had trespassed into your land, they would pretend that they did not understand what you were saying. They would also ensure that you saw the weapon protruding from their *shuka* so as not to leave any doubt in your mind as to what could potentially happen if you spoke out of turn.

With this context in mind, it was not hard to determine that Mwangi was the man cut out for the job. He had an in-depth knowledge of the terrain, James Bond's cunning, and Sherlock Holmes's wit. We commissioned him to proceed with this secret and potentially risky mission. He told us that he would recruit some informers from the neighborhood who would assist with periodic surveillance of the area to monitor all the movements around the property.

We finalized all the arrangements and sent Mwangi on the vital mission. He did not have a pistol but had a torch and an adequate supply of batteries to assure him and his team clear visibility at night as the intruders also tended to trespass into peoples' property at night. He also had a well-sharpened *njora* as a contingency for use in the worst-case scenario.

The wait for the intruders would be long, but eventually, greed would get the better of them. They would make their ill-fated clandestine move about three weeks later, Saturday, July 2, 2016.

SHAMBA SHENANIGANS

We were on an errand to Naivasha town when we received a distress call from spy Mwangi. We immediately abandoned our errand and rushed to the scene of the crime. The communication with Mwangi went something along the following lines:

> *Mwangi: Two young herdsmen have cut the fence. They have shepherded about 20 goats into the shamba. Some of the goats have already started eating trees. Please come immediately.*
>
> *Me: The damn goats! We are coming right away. Please call the Anti-Stock Theft Unit soldiers immediately. And make sure that those thieving goats do not leave the shamba under any circumstances. The soldiers must catch them red-handed.*

It took us about twenty minutes to drive from Naivasha town to Longonot. There are no speed limits in the open savanna grassland, so once we were there, we drove to the crime scene at high speed.

When we reached the shamba, we could not believe our eyes. There were goats all over the place, busy eating our trees and behaving as if Santa Claus had just landed in town. Some goats were moving from tree to tree, munching every morsel of a green leaf on which they could lay their thievish tongues. It was a horrifying sight!

Mwangi, who was now in battle mood, told us that two young herdsboys abandoned the goats and ran away as we were speeding towards the shamba. He had phoned the Anti-Stock Theft Unit soldiers, who said they would come in the next few minutes.

The wait for the soldiers was excruciating. We were worried that the goats would escape before the soldiers had had a chance to witness, first-hand, what was going on.

We watched painfully and helplessly as the goats continued their orgy of destruction. Our intense desire to ensure that the soldiers caught the goats in the act meant that we had to watch in disgust as the goats munched away the young green trees. The physical presence of the goats in the *shamba* was the only evidence that we believed could sustain a case against the perpetrators of the crime. Because of this, we could not chase the goats away. How insane could things get!

We took some photos but were not even sure that such images could suffice as fool-proof evidence in a court of law. It was like watching a house burn down as you waited for the fire brigade, but you could not pour even a single drop of water to control the flames.

The sight evoked a mixture of anger, frustration, and helplessness. But we held tightly onto hope that at least these criminal goats and their masters would at long last be brought to justice.

After about 30 minutes of an agonizing wait, the soldiers arrived in a big, green, mean-looking truck. Initially, we thought that all that the soldiers needed was first-hand visual evidence of the crime in action. Far from it! All the goats that had stepped into the property had to be arrested and taken into custody. That was standard procedure. Indeed, that was the physical evidence that the soldiers needed.

The soldiers started rounding up the goats. It was a fantastic scene. The soldiers would catch a goat on one of its hind legs and heave it onto the truck. Some goats thought they were very smart or too quick for the soldiers, but such thoughts were founded on faulty goat logic.

After apprehending the majority of the goats, the soldiers quickly changed their strategy. They organized themselves into a V-formation and forced the goats to huddle close to each other so that no matter how swiftly a goat tried to escape from the tribe, it was quickly nabbed and heaved onto the truck. Some goats jumped out of the truck in an unbelievably acrobatic fashion but were re-captured rapidly and put back into custody.

The soldiers told us that they would take the goats and keep them in a pen near the base camp. The owner of the goats would invariably own up as they came to fetch the goats. At that point, the soldiers would proffer the relevant charges against the person. The soldiers assured us that the owner would ultimately be required to pay compensation for the damage caused by the goats. Further, this process always yielded the desired results without fail. We were greatly relieved to hear this information.

We thought the drama was over, but we were mistaken. Just as the truck was about to depart, an old *mzee* emerged almost from nowhere, panting profusely. He came running towards the scene of the crime faster than Usain Bolt. It was as if he was running for dear life itself. It turned out that he was the owner of the goats and had mischievously been observing events from his hut about 300 meters away. And when he realized that almost all his earthly possessions were about to be taken away by the soldiers, he abandoned all inhibitions of geezer-hood and ran like a cheetah to retrieve his goats.

He confessed that he owned the goats and that the boys he had sent to herd the goats had disobeyed his instructions and allowed the animals to wander into our property. He pleaded with the soldiers for leniency. But the soldiers would not hear any of that. They asked him to follow them to their base camp to write a statement and be ready for a subsequent court appearance. They were adamant that the law was the law and that everyone, without exception, was required to obey it. The old *mzee* was so shocked by the unexpected turn of events that he started shedding tears.

Susan and I started feeling sorry for the *mzee*. Our annoyance had unexpectedly changed into deep feelings of sympathy. At some point, we started pleading with the soldiers to forgive him. We implored them to release the goats as the *mzee* had expressed deep remorse and sworn never to allow his boys to commit such an offense again.

In a unique turn of events, the old *mzee* asked us to lend him some money to compensate the soldiers for the fuel they had used and the time they had wasted dealing with the issue. We were overcome with sympathy and did not hesitate to hand him some cash. He promised to refund the money in the next few days.

The soldiers released the goats shortly after that. The goats were free to go. It reminded us of the 1966 British drama Born Free. The goats were indeed born free, but what tension they had caused in the savanna grassland of Longonot!

A few days later, we planted trees to replace the damaged ones. Information about the shenanigans with the old *mzee* must have spread around because cases of trespass onto the property reduced dramatically. The old *mzee* never refunded the money he had borrowed from us, but that was not a surprise. It was doubtful that he even ever wanted to see us again.

We were pleased that Mwangi's mission was a success. He proved, without a doubt, that you need not hire James Bond to catch a villain; your unassuming next-door neighbor may turn out to be the best spy in town.

CHAPTER 4

Challenges of a Promising Potato Enterprise

"The way to get started is to quit talking and begin doing."
—Walt Disney

A CONFLUENCE OF GOOD LUCK, exceptionally fertile soils in the highlands of Oraimutia, and sheer determination to bring an ambitious potato farming project to life resulted in a bountiful harvest of potatoes. However, the onset of heavy rains changed the dynamics of the entire enterprise virtually overnight. The economic outcome of the enterprise was devastating, but the life lessons were immense.

❖❖❖

SOMETIME IN 2007, SUSAN AND I visited uncle Ndungu at Nyahururu. We were so impressed by the pristine and magical countryside of Nyahururu that we decided to start saving money to buy some land in that area. And as Paulo Coelho narrates so vividly in The Alchemist, when you aspire for something and take action to pursue it, all the world will conspire to bring your ambitions to reality (Coelho, 2012).

In about two years, we had raised some money to supplement a loan from a Savings and Credit Society to buy a piece of land in Nyahururu. From that point on, we spent the next ten weekends in different parts of the beautiful Nyahururu countryside looking for suitable land under the able guidance of local real estate agents Kamau, Pele, and Jacko.

The search for land was well choreographed. We would meet with Kamau, Pele, and Jacko at a designated spot in Nyahururu town. The team would give us details of the land that was available for sale. We would then select three or four locations to visit. After touring the properties, we would return to Nyahururu town in the late afternoon. We would have lunch, which was always roast goat meat or fried chicken, accompanied by sumptuous portions of ugali or chips. We would then debrief on the site visits and agree to meet the following weekend to do the same thing. We repeated this ritual about ten times before settling on land at Oraimutia, about 15 kilometers from Nyahururu town.

The land was located in literally virgin territory and was suitable for almost any type of agricultural production, particularly potatoes. After going through the legal process of acquiring the land, Susan and I were ready to try our hand at a large-scale potato farming venture.

SHAMBA SHENANIGANS

It was a challenge getting people to till the land properly. An even more significant difficulty was getting the required quantity of potato seeds. We approached the Ministry of Agriculture at Oljororok. Mureithi, one of the agricultural officers there, talked to us at great length about the ins and outs of potato farming. We were surprised to learn about the multiple varieties of potatoes grown in Kenya. There were more than 30 of them, but the most commonly grown in our county, Nyandarua County, were *Tigoni*, *Shangi*, and *Nyayo*. Mureithi recommended that we buy seeds that were already certified by the Kenya Plant Health Inspectorate Service (KEPHIS). He even introduced us to his relatives and other potato farmers in the area, who happily supplied us with the potato seeds we needed.

We proceeded with the venture with enthusiasm. We felt that we had finally found an opening in agribusiness that seemed potentially lucrative. The planting and tending of the potato farm went well. And because we were farming on virgin land, the production was excellent.

The field, blooming with purple flowers of *Shangi* potato plants, was a magical sight to behold. There was something spiritual about it. The weekend trips to Nyahururu to inspect the potato farm were almost like pilgrimages to a holy land. These trips were enormously fulfilling.

The harvest was superb. We filled a big store with high-quality *Shangi* potatoes, ready for sale.

As the harvesting was going on, Susan and I thought of what we believed was a brilliant idea. Instead of selling the potatoes directly from the shamba, we would hire a transporter to carry them to Marigiti, the largest market in Nairobi then, where we were bound to sell the potatoes at excellent prices.

But before hiring a transporter, we thought it prudent to visit Marigiti to look for a market for our potatoes and to establish the necessary business contacts. After all, our home in Nairobi was only a 30-minute drive to the Marigiti market.

Things were moving rather fast, and we did not want to wait until the weekend to visit. We had to do it during the weekday. The visit to Marigiti would not be a problem because the business there was transacted very early in the morning. We had learned that transporters delivered the produce from up-country from around 2:00 am. So, there was an opportunity to do our pre-sale visit and still have time for a shower at home before proceeding to work for our day jobs.

We went to Marigiti on a Monday in the wee hours. When we got there, we realized, to our amazement, that it was perhaps the busiest place on earth. There were trucks upon trucks carrying different varieties of potatoes and other types of agricultural produce from different parts of the country. Some vehicles carried produce imported from Tanzania and Uganda. It was an incredible sight.

Wielding our way through the trucks amidst the loud noise and the hordes of people carrying sacks on their shoulders was an almost life-threatening experience. We spoke to a few traders who appeared less busy than the others. We learned that there was an established closely-knit network of transporters, traders, truck off-loaders, cart drivers, and the local authorities who issued permits to the people conducting business in the market.

On the surface, it looked like the most chaotic operation we had ever witnessed, but clearly, there was order beneath the apparent chaos. One had to be a member of the closely-knit network to understand it.

The numerous middlemen seemed to recognize newcomers instantly. The manner of dress of newcomers was bound to give them away. Once the astute Marigiti operatives marked you as newcomers, they would immediately know how best to handle you, as we came to learn later.

Almost everyone seemed engrossed in one activity or another. We had carried a sample of potatoes from our shamba. We showed the sample to the first person who seemed interested. His first question was to know the source of the potatoes. We told him that they were from Oraimutia in Nyandarua County. He looked at the potatoes and said that we were out of luck because, at that particular time, most of his customers in Nairobi were only interested in potatoes from Mau Narok. He suggested that we try our luck with other traders in the market.

When we spoke to the next trader, we worked hard to focus his attention on the large size of our potatoes, but there were challenges. He was willing to buy our potatoes, but at a discount, apparently, because his customers had a particular dislike for the size size "B" (1.5 inches in diameter) potatoes that we were offering. His customers preferred the larger "A" (2.5 inches in diameter) potatoes, which were better for making chips. We spoke to several other traders, but none of them was ready to offer us prices that we considered reasonable to warrant the hassle of hiring a transporter to carry our potatoes from Oraimutia to Marigiti.

It was a harsh environment for beginners. We got the sense that one had to have a certain inborn sense of ferociousness and street-smartness to survive. It would not be easy for Susan and me to immerse ourselves in that complicated world. We did not have the flexibility or time to learn the ropes; neither did we think it was the right thing to do given the demands of our regular day jobs. Accordingly, we decided to stick to the more straightforward side of the value chain and sell our potatoes at the farm level, despite the lower prices.

As I drove to work later that morning and reflected on my experience earlier that morning, it struck me that I had been to a different world that existed hardly ten kilometers from our home. A little later, as I entered the lift to go to my office, I felt a sense of immense bliss as if I traveled in a special craft to the clouds. After alighting from the elevator and entering the office, I met some of my workmates. Their faces looked immensely fresh. They looked like beautiful birds that were waiting for me at the gates of Shangri-La. I then saw two other beautiful birds emerging from the direction of the marketing department. Both of them were in gorgeous tight dresses and high-heeled shoes. For a moment, my mind returned to Marigiti, and I wondered how the ladies would survive in that kind of environment. It was evident that we lived in two parallel worlds.

SHAMBA SHENANIGANS

I was exceptionally productive in the office that day, perhaps a tribute to the knowledge of how lucky I was as an office worker. I started seeing things from a different perspective. The office environment now seemed amazingly orderly. Everyone seemed courteous. There was hardly any noise nor incessant haggling amongst the people. No cladding with multiple pieces of clothing to shield oneself from cold weather. Just peace! Peaceful dialogue with my workmates in low tones. How wonderful!

However, upon further reflection, it also occurred to me that the alternative type of work at Marigiti also had unique benefits. For example, I would spend the next eight hours in front of my computer, while many of the people I left at Marigiti would be relaxing at home with their families. They would probably also watch their favorite shows on television later in the day and witness different news events as they unfolded first-hand on their television screens, as they waited for the next piece of the action at 2:00 am on the following day.

◆◆◆

Towards the tail end of the harvesting period at Oraimutia, it started raining heavily. It rained, rained, and rained. It was as if all water taps in the heavens had been left open. And then! The wonder of wonders happened. We learned that roads in the area had become entirely impassable by trucks because of the heavy rains. The roads department in the county government had completely forgotten Oraimutia. Buyers of potatoes could not make it to the farms.

Here we were with tons and tons of potatoes but with nowhere to take them. The joy of an abundant harvest slowly turned into doubt, doubt into anxiety, and anxiety into frustration. And then, as if from nowhere, sweet-talking potato brokers started emerging, one at a time.

A potato broker is a particular anthropomorphic living entity with all the human traits except one – a sense of fairness. These brokers were ready to buy our potatoes, despite the challenges of transportation, which they knew how to navigate, as long as we allowed them to set the buying price. It was like somebody walking into a high-end clothing store in Nairobi and saying to the shop manager, "I will buy all the suits in your shop, but you must sell them to me at KShs 1,000/= (US$ 10) each."

After interacting with three of these brokers and indignantly dismissing each of them, we realized that they were part of a cartel. The cartel's sole mission was to make as much money as humanly possible for themselves, even if it meant leaving a trail of financially obliterated potato farmers.

The last few interactions with these brokers were particularly tricky. One of them offered to buy the potatoes at KShs 900/= per bag. We angrily declined the offer, which we said was an insult to the farmer, given that market prices in Nairobi were around KShs 3,000/= per bag. There was no way that we could accept such a low offer. The broker left nonchalantly, looking surprisingly calm. A few days later, another broker emerged almost unannounced. He offered KShs 800/= per bag and would not budge when we asked him to raise it to at least KShs 850/=, given that the previous broker had offered KShs 900/=. He argued vigorously that market prices had dropped during the preceding week and that there was no way that he could afford to pay even a single cent above KShs 800/=. We parted ways without even some fake smiles.

Potatoes have a maximum shelf-life of around two weeks when appropriately stored at average room temperature. Refrigeration can extend the shelf life to three months. We did not have any cooling system since electric power was not available in that area. The situation was, therefore, becoming desperate by the day. As desperation slowly started turning into despair, the king of all potato brokers made an appearance.

The king of potato brokers was exceptionally diplomatic. He presented himself as the saint of all potato farmers of Oraimutia. His verve and sophistication seemed quite out of character in the rural setting. He was like a breath of fresh air.

However, our hopes of a decent bargain quickly evaporated the moment he mentioned his offer. He was ready to buy our entire stock of potatoes at KShs 700/= per bag. He assured us that this price was better than any other broker on planet earth could offer at that time, especially given the poor state of the road network in Oraimutia.

It became apparent that he was one of them, and he knew full well that they, the cartel, had succeeded in putting us in a tight corner where they wanted us to remain. We had no choice. Out of sheer desperation, we sold the potatoes to him at KShs 750/= per bag. When we closed the sale, little did we know that there was yet another deep emotional chasm that was about to test our sanity as entrepreneurs in agribusiness.

When we agreed to sell our potatoes at KShs 750/= per bag, we did not realize that the word "bag of potatoes" actually had a special meaning in Oraimutia. In this part of the world, a bag meant one 90-kg "bag of potatoes," plus another half of a 90-kg "bag of potatoes" on top, with the two bags sown skillfully together. Finally, a net was attached on top of the elongated "bag of potatoes" to create space for an additional ten or so kilograms of potatoes, forming a nice ice-cream cone-like curvy shape at the top of the "bag of potatoes." Now, this was the full Oraimutia "bag of potatoes."

A normal human being could not carry one well-packed Oraimutia "bag of potatoes." And all Oraimutia "bags of potatoes" were exceptionally well-packed. Lifting one of these bags onto a truck required the collective effort of three well-fed men. This packaging was a clear example of extortion at its worst!

But we had no choice. We sold the potatoes to the broker at what was, in essence, a pittance. On that day, we said "*au revoir pomme de terre*" to large-scale potato farming until the government improved the road network in Oraimutia and set regulations on the packaging of potatoes.

This venture taught us that while one's entrepreneurial spirit is essential, it is not the only thing that counts in agribusiness. Some basic research on all aspects of the value chain is vital. Also, before you sign a potato sales contract in Oraimutia, make sure you fully understand what the phrase "a bag of potatoes" really means.

CHAPTER 5

Hay and Debris

*"You only live once, but if you do it
right, once is enough."*
—Mae West

THERE IS A FARM IN Njoro that prides itself on rearing the best quality cows, thanks to modern technological dairy farming techniques that include almost human-like grooming of cows. We discovered the farm as we were looking for hay for our cows. The farm sold us both hay and debris. However, the farm manager's ownership and accountability was a lesson to be emulated by others.

◆◆◆

AFTER BURNING OUR FINGERS IN the potato farming venture, we started growing other crops, such as maize and beans, but there was little excitement in these other crops.

We bought a few sheep too. They began multiplying, but the growth in numbers was slowed down by barbecues that had become an increasingly regular feature during the weekend visits to the shamba at Oraimutia.

The barbecues, in the company of family and friends below beautiful bright blue skies, were occasions we could not trade for anything. Seeing sheep grazing in the open fields on a beautiful sunny day was one of the most fulfilling experiences. But it was time to try something else that would make the shamba commercially viable, even if it was just to break even.

When we were going through the agonies of the potato agribusiness, we also followed a weekly agricultural show on television. In one of the shows, the host created the impression that dairy farming was the best thing that had happened to humankind since emergence from the Stone Age. He made viewers believe that dairy farmers all over Kenya were laughing all the way to the bank every day.

There was only one glaring inconsistency. None of the dairy farmers we had met ever talked about big money from dairy farming. And if indeed they were getting much money from it, they must have been secretly emulating the frugality of one of the wealthiest and most prudent business people in the world, Warren Buffet. We knew that Warren Buffet drove a simple Cadillac despite being one of the most significant shareholders of General Motors, one of the largest car manufacturing companies in the world. Before jumping into the lucrative dairy farming enterprise, we needed to understand this apparent inconsistency.

SHAMBA SHENANIGANS

The answers to our uncertainties came unexpectedly from one of our friends, Chege. It is not easy to remember what triggered the conversation about dairy farming. But many people had been watching the fascinating stories on T.V., and anyone with even a modicum of interest in agribusiness was yearning to go into dairy farming - to make big money. One episode of the T.V. show profiled a young technology expert who had abandoned his calling in IT to pursue dairy farming and had, in less than a year, started taking money to the bank in gunny bags. Therefore, with this context, it was not a wonder that we had begun talking about dairy farming with Chege. He invited us to visit one of his relatives who had been doing dairy farming for some time at Githunguri. We accepted the invitation and went there one Saturday afternoon.

The farmer practiced zero grazing for his cows on land less than half an acre in size. He kept a herd of about 15 milking cows, plus several calves of different ages. We were impressed by the clean, neat, and well-maintained pens. He told us that his milk production was quite high compared to other farmers in Githunguri who had larger farms. Going by his tremendous enthusiasm and his confident gait as he showed us around the premises, it was apparent that he was pleased with his dairy farming enterprise. The farmer enjoyed a significant competitive edge over the other farmers because of his access to spent malt, *macica*, which he collected from the Kenya Breweries factory at Ruaraka twice a week.

◆◆◆

According to the Food and Agriculture Organization of the United Nations, spent malt is a good source of energy and protein. It can serve as a valuable supplementary feed for livestock when properly stored. Further, it is a balanced diet for cows and stimulates milk production (FAO, 2019).

The use of *macica* enabled the farmer to enhance the milk production of his cows. However, we could not help thinking that high milk production was a function of the slightly intoxicating ingredients in the *macica* that probably induced the cows to release the brakes in their mammary glands.

◆◆◆

The visit to the Githunguri dairy farm was the trigger that we were expecting. I persuaded Susan that we should consider venturing into the dairy farming business right way. We then jumped into it with gusto.

We were keen to start the venture properly to enhance the chances of success. There was no room for error. Accordingly, we determined that hiring a well-qualified farm manager was a critical success factor. We pursued several leads and eventually met Kamau. He was a qualified veterinarian, a qualification that would be of immense advantage in a dairy farm. We hired him on a full-time basis. He was a bit expensive by Oraimutia standards, but we were ready to make the necessary sacrifices to start the venture on the right footing.

SHAMBA SHENANIGANS

Kamau helped us buy six milking cows. Two Friesians from Kinangop that we named Eldoret and Dubai, and another expensive but beautiful Friesian from his friend in Naivasha that we named Maridadi. Two small Masai cows from Naivasha that we named Musaka and Maruti. Finally, a Guernsey from another friend of his at Karagita, near Lake Naivasha, we named Fiona.

We bought Fiona from an exceptionally entrepreneurial farmer who had taken zero-grazing to a whole new level. First of all, there was no cowshed on his premises. He lived in a small tin house. The cow had a rope tied to one of its hind legs, and the other end of the rope tied to a wooden pole outside the home. The farmer fed the cow with freshly cut green grass sourced from the periphery of a nearby airstrip. Despite the unconventional living quarters, seeing how extraordinarily healthy Fiona looked was quite inspiring.

Transporting the cows to the shamba was an exciting experience. We moved them in two batches. The first delivery of two cows was uneventful. However, for the next delivery, the lorry got stuck in the mud about five kilometers from the shamba. The cows were offloaded and shepherded to the shamba through a thick forest.

There was a sacred pact amongst locals that any time anyone saw a herd of cows passing through the forest, the person was required to inform all the other farmers. This communication was essential in case thieves had stolen the cows from one of the farmers. Incidents of theft were infrequent, but farmers were diligent in sharing information on any suspicious activity.

As our cows were moving through the forest, one of our neighbors called to alert us about the suspicious herd. We assured him the cows belonged to us and the neighbors did not need to worry.

Three of the cows reached the shamba without much difficulty. Maridadi, on the other hand, utterly refused to cross a footbridge over a river about one kilometer from the shamba. No amount of persuasion or intimidation would convince the cow to cross the bridge. The cow was several months pregnant and had spent most of its life in a zero-grazing environment. It somehow could not muster enough courage to walk on the footbridge. All this was happening as darkness was beginning to set in. So, we hired somebody to watch over the cow overnight. Perhaps out of sheer exhaustion and hunger, Maridadi finally crossed the river the following morning.

The initial stages of the dairy farming venture went well. Kamau fed the cows well. The milk production of 60Kgs per day was reasonable. The production increased gradually to around 80kgs after four months. Whenever we visited the shamba, we returned to Nairobi carrying several jugs of fresh milk that we would sometimes share with friends and relatives; and refrigerated a large quantity for our home consumption.

We enjoyed the milk a lot, perhaps because of the knowledge that it had come directly from our cows.

SHAMBA SHENANIGANS

Kamau inseminated the cows with imported hybrid semen. He was an expert in this exercise. He had his artificial insemination kit that included a sophisticated stainless-steel container, forceps, a straw gun, and other paraphernalia. He would order the semen from a particular supplier in Naivasha town. He would collect the semen two or so days later and store it in the aluminum container. When he opened the vessel even slightly, a sensational white smoke would emerge, the kind of smoke that one saw in magic shows.

The price of the imported gender-selected semen was quite high, KShs 12,000/= per 1/4 cc straw, compared to KShs 1,000/= for the local variety. There was no way of determining whether what went into the container was imported or local. We trusted the supplier and relied on the professionalism of Kamau.

We learned that the white smoke from the container was liquid nitrogen that preserved the semen at low dry temperatures before insemination. It was probably also intended to create a certain sense of pizzazz for buyers of the semen. You didn't just pay KShs 12,000/= or KShs 1,000/= for such a little quantity of something without getting to enjoy a magic show to demonstrate that your purchase was worth it. Some abracadabra was essential.

The expenses of the dairy business continued to rise. The income, on the other hand, remained almost stagnant. It reached a point where we could no longer afford the salary we were paying Kamau. Accordingly, we were unable to renew his contract when it expired.

We were not experts in animal husbandry. But from our perspective, the artificial insemination did not seem to result in calves with exceptional qualities. When the calves grew into mature milking cows, our hopes of high milk production turned out to be mere pipe dreams. The good news was that in just four years, the size of the flock had increased significantly.

We developed a rudimentary cow naming convention. The convention was linked to significant events playing out locally, nationally, or internationally or the names of individuals at the center of those events when a calf was born. Using this convention, we ended up with a herd of many superstars after just a few years. It included Obama, Michelle, and even Mandela. There was Uhuru, Ruto, and Clinton too.

Other memorable but relatively nondescript members of the herd were Judy, named after one of our relatives, and Germany. The name Germany was a tribute to the German football team that won the FIFA 2014 World Cup. We called another cow Snow in memory of a highly unusual event in February 2015 at Kinangop, not far from Oraimutia, when a beautiful blanket of snow covered the main road and the countryside. We named another cow after one of my sisters, who graced us with a visit to the farm in late 2015.

We later sold off Mandela, Musaka, Uhuru, Obama, and Jubilee, all of which had grown into wonderful big fat bulls. The sales proceeds helped us reduce the accumulated losses. Judy, Michelle, and Joy grew into marvelous milk producers.

During the dry seasons, the expenses of the dairy farm skyrocketed. The need to buy hay from external sources caused the most significant cost increase, which led us to Technology Farm in Njoro.

Technology Farm is a sister institution of the Rift Valley Institute of Science & Technology. The farm occupies a vast piece of land in Njoro. The farm grows hay, which it uses to feed its cows and sell to outsiders. The farm employs some of the latest technologies in dairy farming. For example, in the May 9, 2016 edition of the online magazine Farmers Trend, the manager of the farm is quoted as having said that "The cows are bathed at least once a week, their hooves are trimmed regularly while those on a pilot zero-grazing project have bedding" (Sally, Paul, & Beth, 2018). How wonderful!

On February 21, 2019, we bought 300 bales of hay from Technology Farm. We hired a truck to transport the hay to the shamba the same day. We called Mzee Inziani, who took care of the cows. We asked him to start feeding the cows with the hay from Technology Farm the next day.

Two days later, Mzee Inziani telephoned us in a state of panic. He said the cows had refused to eat the hay from Technology Farm. After receiving that information, the first thought that came to mind was that it was probably a temporary phenomenon attributable to the sudden change in diet as the cows were previously grazing in an open field. However, Mzee Inziani was insistent that the hay was of inferior quality. We asked him to try his best to find alternative feed until we got a chance to view the hay and figured out the best way forward.

Two days later, we went to the shamba, by which time Mzee Inziani had unwrapped several bales. We noticed to our utter dismay that approximately 50% of the bales contained hay mixed with all sorts of debris, including small thorny branches of acacia trees. Some bales contained traces of cow dung too. This situation was highly distressing. We could hardly bring ourselves to appreciate the suffering the cows must have gone through during the two days they had painfully tried to feed on the hay. How could the Technology Farm descend to such a low level?

I wrote a letter to the Manager of the Technology Farm complaining about the horrible and unacceptable situation. The Manager called me two days later. He apologized profusely and explained that the people at Technology Farm who had loaded the truck had picked the hay from the wrong batch.

He told me the tractors used for hay harvesting also collected the farm debris at the end of the harvesting season. It was a routine clean-up exercise, he said. The harvesters packed the waste into bales, just like the regular hay. The debris was subsequently thrown into the cowsheds to soften the floors that the cows walked on. Somebody in the sales department had inadvertently issued us with waste instead of hay.

The manager talked to me courteously and professionally, apologizing for the colossal mistake almost at every turn. I believed him. He organized for a replacement of the debris with good-quality hay.

We much appreciated the responsiveness and professionalism of the Technology Farm manager. Faced with a similar moral dilemma, people in other institutions would probably have reacted differently to avoid being accountable for their mistakes.

◆◆◆

Despite its weakness as a commercially viable venture, we continued with our hobby of dairy farming. However, we tried our best to keep the number of cows in the herd as small as possible.

There was something unusually relaxing about being around beautiful animals, especially when they were grazing innocently in the open green fields, more than 150 kilometers away from the hustle and bustle of Nairobi. That was something that money could not buy.

As I relaxed in the open fields watching the cows and sheep graze, many different thoughts went through my mind. At one time, it struck me that the life of a cow or a sheep was quite interesting. These animals seemed to be motivated by two simple things: food and water. Compared to human beings, they appeared entirely comfortable at only one level of Maslow's hierarchy of needs (Maslow, 1943): the need to satisfy physiological needs.

The cows and sheep never seemed to get enough of the physiological needs. For example, when they woke up in the morning, they waited anxiously for Mzee Inziani to take them to the green fields. When they were released and reached the fields, they just ate grass continuously, with only the occasional break for water consumption.

It was interesting to see how some sheep would surreptitiously sneak out from the herd and wander into vegetable gardens neighboring the grazing fields when Mzee Inziani was not paying attention. This behavior would infuriate Mzee Inziani. He would spend the next few minutes chasing the sheep and re-directing them back into the grazing area. These occasional dramatic events were quite entertaining.

The almost insatiable desire for food also meant that the cows did not give their milk voluntarily. To go into the milking shed, a cow had to be enticed with small portions of nice tasting dairy meal. And when the cow got into the shed, its hind legs had to be tied tightly with a rope to allow Mzee Inziani to safely milk it with his bare hands. Failure to secure the hind legs was asking for trouble, as the cow would invariably unleash one or so dangerous kicks during the milking process, tipping the milking bucket and spilling all the precious milk on the ground.

Regarding Maslow's hierarchy of needs, there were times when I wondered whether my assumptions about the needs of the animals were correct. If someone were to construct a hierarchy of animal needs, would it include the need for security, I wondered? Probably yes, given how Maridadi behaved despite the intense persuasion to encourage it to cross a bridge when it arrived in Oraimutia. Would the hierarchy include the need for social belonging? Probably yes, given how our sheep always seemed to huddle together when grazing. Would it include the need for self-esteem? Perhaps, given how badly Malewa behaved when other cows tried to occupy a space it had claimed for itself in the cowshed. It was a cow with an enormous ego. We had to create a partition in the cowshed to keep the cow separate from the other cows to avoid any incidents of cow violence.

Would the animal hierarchy of needs include self-actualization? In other words, the need for a cow or sheep to be the best animal they could be. That was a question for debate.

Turning back to the economics of dairy farming, Susan and I often wondered how Kenyans who relied on dairy farming for their livelihood made ends meet. It was one of the few enterprises where prices of the finished product remained stagnant for several years while production expenses continued to rise.

Indeed, even as this book is going to press, dairy farmers in some parts of the country are up in arms because of a recent sharp decline in the farm prices of milk (Parliament of Kenya Senate Hansard, 2019). They claim, and they are right, that the farmers' selling price of one liter of milk is now lower than the price of one liter of water. Further, dairy farmers' bonuses from the milk processing companies in respect of 2018 milk deliveries were at record low levels. Our experience regarding the 2018 milk bonus may help illustrate the farmers' agony.

Many milk processing companies that buy milk from farmers usually retain a small amount of money from the farmers' dues on daily milk deliveries. At the end of the fiscal year, the dairy company pays farmers the amount retained after deducting costs incurred by the dairy company on their behalf. The payment is called a "bonus." Farmers usually look forward to the annual bonus payment with great anticipation.

In mid-2019, we received periodic messages via SMS from Ol Kalou Dairy Company, reminding us to collect from their offices our bonus for 2018 milk deliveries. So, sometime in October 2019, we decided to go there to collect the bonus.

The road trip from Nairobi to Ol Kalou Dairy took about three and a half hours. When we got there, Susan spoke to one of the Accountants to inquire about the bonus. The Accountant handed her a small hand-written note with the number 1911 written on it and asked her to proceed to a nearby bank to collect the bonus. Susan assumed that 1911 was a reference number for the bonus payment. She excitedly went to the bank as instructed and joined the bonus payments queue.

The queue was moving very slowly. So, out of anxiety, considering the distance we had traveled to collect the bonus, Susan decided to seek guidance from a lady at the Customer Service Desk on alternative ways of accessing the money. In discussion with the lady, it turned out that the number on the hand-written note from the Accountant represented the amount of bonus we were entitled to, KShs 1,911/= (US$ 19). Susan was dumbfounded. After making milk deliveries for a whole year, we were the lucky recipients of a bonus that could buy only six bales of hay.

Additionally, we had traveled 160 kilometers for three and a half hours to collect a milk bonus of KShs 1,911/= (US$ 19). Why would the dairy company not have just sent us the money via electronic bank transfer?

The dairy farming enterprise was a perfect example of the risks of jumping onto a bandwagon. In effect, we hopped onto a train that we believed would take us to the land of milk, butter, and cheese, but we ended at a different destination in Oraimutia. But we found other things about dairy farming more valuable than money. For example, the immense feeling of tranquility we would experience while resting in the open green fields on a sunny day and watching the cows graze.

CHAPTER 6

Charcoal Burning Venture Beats Cash Crops

> *"Our greatest glory is not in never falling, but in rising every time we fall."*
> —Oliver Goldsmith

AS WE CONTINUED WITH THE twists and turns of dairy farming in Oraimutia; we got involved in other different farming activities at Matathia, closer to Nairobi, on a small piece of land. That would turn out to be another exciting journey with valuable life lessons. For example, we had never imagined that selling charcoal would be more lucrative than selling bulb onions. We learned this commercial lesson in many interesting and unexpected ways, thanks to the ingenuity and entrepreneurial acumen of Kangethe.

◆◆◆

FUNDIS IN MATATHIA HAVE A certain kind of positive entrepreneurial spirit that is very difficult to describe. It is a positive attitude you may never find anywhere else in the business world.

As we started preparing the small shamba at Matathia, we met a carpenter called Kangethe. We later came to learn that he was a jack of all trades.

When Kangethe finished building a small wooden house for us at the shamba, he was full of other ideas on how we could generate endless streams of money. One of his suggestions was that if we planted *dhanias* on a quarter of an acre, we would make more money than Warren Buffet, Bill Gates, and Jeff Bezos combined.

We immediately commissioned him to clear one section of the shamba covered with black wattle trees so that we could use the space for the *dhanias* project. He reached out to the local Chief for a permit and sourced the services of a lumberjack to cut down the trees.

We intended to use the felled trees as firewood. However, Kangethe quickly brought it to our attention that at that very moment, we were looking at the ingredients of pure black gold. All that we needed to do was turn the felled trees into charcoal.

That was not all. Kangethe was an expert charcoal burner too and would do the job at a minimal cost. Kangethe's proposition sounded like winning the maximum prize from one spin of the slot machine at the casino.

SHAMBA SHENANIGANS

We kicked off the charcoal burning project in earnest. It involved cutting the felled black wattle trees into small stumps, approximately three feet long. The stumps were then arranged nicely into several heaps. Dry and wet leaves were then inserted between the tree stumps. The heaps were then completely covered with soil to form mounds. A small opening was left at one end of each mound into which fire was introduced, and the wood in the mound left to burn slowly for several days.

Kangethe and his team inspected the mounds periodically to ensure that there was no part of a mound where the soil had collapsed, creating gaps through which air could enter the mound. Such air vents caused the wood to burn at an accelerated rate and form ashes rather than charcoal. The vents were therefore covered with additional soil expeditiously. Checking the mounds was a delicate exercise requiring considerable caution and particular expertise.

After five days, Kangethe and his team carefully uncovered the mounds to retrieve the black gold that had formed through some alchemy. The black gold was charcoal.

Some tree stumps in some mounds had not burnt to the required degree. Fresh soil was added to these mounds, and the tree stumps were left to continue burning to form the beautiful black gold.

Cold water was poured on the mounds that were ready. The charcoal was then retrieved and packed into gunny bags. The charcoal in each gunny bag was then covered with a layer of green leaves at the top, and the mouth of the bag was sewn with strings made from the green bark of young black wattle trees. The fully packed bags of charcoal were then arranged in an orderly fashion, ready for sale. Kangethe managed all stages of the charcoal burning and packing process with immense diligence.

Selling the charcoal turned out to be the most lucrative "agribusiness" venture we had ever conducted. The demand for charcoal was beyond belief. Local villagers and passers-by, including matatus transporting passengers to Kimende town, would stop by to inquire about the charcoal and place advance orders. Susan and I did not quite understand what drove the high demand in the first two days.

At the end of day two, we carried one bag of charcoal for our use at home in Nairobi. It was during the cold season, and with the abundance of charcoal at our disposal, it made sense to use some of it to warm our house. That evening, when we lighted the charcoal *jiko* at our home in Nairobi, we quickly realized what drove the high demand. It was an astounding revelation.

Charcoal made from the black wattle tree is slow-burning and produces a red-hot flame that generates heat over an extended period. It is incomparable to charcoal from most other types of trees in Matathia.

We telephoned Kangethe that very night and asked him to reserve no less than ten bags of charcoal for our personal use. It took time to convince him to accept these directives as he had already taken advance orders from countless people in the Matathia village. However, through some arm-twisting, we convinced him to shift things around and reserve five bags. There was an unpleasant exchange of words at some point, but we did not take it seriously. After all, it was Kangethe who had come up with the idea of the charcoal business in the first place.

The cash flow was good. Therefore, I needed to closely monitor the daily transactions to avoid any cash leakages. You would have thought that counting bulky items using the basic 1, 2, and 3 arithmetical approach was straightforward. In this particular instance, one had to stretch simple arithmetic to the limits.

Different activities were happening at various locations in the shamba. A few people were busy opening up some mounds; others were pouring water on other freshly opened mounds, while others were retrieving and sorting charcoal from the piles that had cooled down. Others were packing charcoal into gunny bags, while others were moving the fully-loaded bags into different locations within the shamba to simplify management of the inventory.

Sales activity was happening at the same time. Some customers seemed hell-bent on creating confusion by selecting bags from different mounds in a quest to purchase the bags with the maximum amount of charcoal in them. Some customers would even stand near a freshly opened mound waiting for the bags to be packed.

Managing the inventory and sales transactions in the first two days was simple. At that time, there was no need for complexities of purchase orders, delivery notes, sales invoices, and the like. It was easy to keep track of the transactions in memory. But after a short while, things started changing dramatically. Order quickly turned into almost utter chaos.

> One Kamau from Kimende would call Kangethe and place an order for ten bags to be collected the following day. As a commitment to the purchase, Kamau would pay a deposit of about 20%. Meanwhile, Mama Njeri and Mama Lucy from the village would show up. Mama Njeri would pay for three bags, one of which she would carry on the spot; her son Kimani to collect the other two bags later that afternoon. Mama Lucy would buy one bag plus two bags of the discounted low-grade variety. Karanja, another local farmer, would send his daughter to buy three bags. He would pay for two of them, with the balance to be paid at the end of the week when he received money from his sale of dhanias. He was two or so decades older than Kangethe and would leverage his age to compel Kangethe to reserve the remaining bag for him and two more. At around the same time, Thuo would arrive to collect three of the five bags his elder brother had bought the previous day and only paid KShs 2,000/=. And so on, ad infinitum.

I would keep a close eye on charcoal collections to ensure that there was proper accounting for every bag. I would get a little confused at some point, but Kangethe would magically shed light with such absolute clarity that it made me feel a bit dazzled. For example:

> *How could I not remember that Mama Njambi, a distant relative of mine on my mother's side, had ordered five bags the day before and paid for two in cash and one via M-Pesa? Had collected two sacks, was now ready to receive two more? And needed to obtain the remaining bag the following day, with the sole intent of clearing the entire outstanding debt by Friday on her way to deliver milk to her customers at Mwimutoni?*

I would nod knowingly, but at the bottom of my heart, I would know that that nod would perhaps have cost me a whole bag of charcoal.

"And who is that walking away with one bag on his shoulders?" I would ask. Kangethe would, in turn, shout, threateningly at the top of his voice, at the gentleman who was carrying the bag and who was just on the verge of exiting the shamba unnoticed, "*Wee! Niurihite?*" ("You! Have you paid?") Kangethe's quick thinking, along with the shout, would have, in effect, nipped an act of potential impropriety in the bud.

The cash inflow was good, but the toll in the continual adrenalin rush was too much! I became fully convinced that things did not get this complicated when the British colonial government was building the Lunatic Express from the port of Mombasa to Kampala in the 18th century, who had to contend with a significant language barrier and the man-eating lions of Tsavo.

After two days of almost utter chaos, it was time to call on the wisdom of the early-medieval Romans and Jews who invented the double-entry accounting system (Parker, 1989); and the genius of the Franciscan Friar Luca Pacioli, who ably memorialized it in *Summa de arithmetica* (Ghaligai & Pacioli, 1521). The underlying reasons for these early sages' actions became vividly clear during those few days at Matathia. Accordingly, I introduced a simple bookkeeping system that helped bring some sanity into the operation.

◆◆◆

The charcoal business lasted about three weeks. It was a good enterprise with excellent cash flow and profitability. It was also a great service to the people of Matathia, who enjoyed the warm energy from excellent charcoal from the black wattle tree during a time when average daily temperatures would drop as low as 8 degrees Celsius.

◆◆◆

When the charcoal business was over, it was time to prepare the land for growing cash crops. It turned out that Kangethe was not just a carpenter and charcoal burner but also an expert in growing *dhanias*.

Before embarking on this project, Kangethe was full of praise for the dhania business. He told us that buyers would be coming to the shamba in droves and that we would be dictating the selling price, just as we did for the charcoal business.

He showed us how to plant *dhanias*. The trick was to till the soil thoroughly until it became soft and completely free of weeds before planting and keeping the *dhanias* watered regularly, something that Kangethe himself volunteered to do, a rather expensive exercise for us, but it seemed to be worth it.

Kangethe undertook the implementation of the *dhanias* project with great enthusiasm. However, when the *dhanias* were ready for harvesting, we did not see hordes of buyers. He explained that the market for *dhanias* was a little subdued because food suppliers to schools were the main buyers, and at that time, schools had been closed for holidays.

We learned a little later that many other farmers had planted *dhanias* during that same period, resulting in a massive glut in the market. It turned out to be a loss-making venture, but at least we learned a lot about the ins and outs of dhania farming.

◆◆◆

Kangethe's enthusiasm and agribusiness acumen were commendable. Almost out of the blue, he came up with yet another idea. He told us that onions were the in-thing. People were going bonkers from the profits of this business. There was some truth in it. Farm prices for white bulb onions had reached KShs 120/= per kilogram, an excellent price indeed. Onion farmers had truly hit the jackpot. Buyers would flock to the shambas looking for white bulb onions.

Therefore, it did not take much for Kangethe to convince us to go into onions. He told us that he looked forward to the day when we would sit comfortably on benches at the entrance to the shamba, waiting for buyers to finish harvesting the onions. The buyers would also pack the onions and dutifully present the packaged product to us to determine the price and pay us in cash. He speculated that when that time came, we would remember him and reward him handsomely.

We bought the best onion seeds in the market and embarked on our journey into the onions' agribusiness with high expectations. The yields were excellent. But Beelzebub is never far away during times of a good harvest. The market price for white bulb onions suddenly dropped to KShs 55/= per kilogram. Many buyers approached us to buy our produce at this price, but we declined their offers. We suspected that they were trying to fleece us because we were new in the business. After some time, we moderated our ambitions. We started offering the onions at KShs 60/= per kilogram, but there were no takers. The price continued to drop. Somebody offered us KShs 50/=, but we turned it down too. The prices continued to fall.

The beauty of onions was that one could store them for up to six months. This attribute was a significant advantage. We had the option of holding out for as long as possible to ensure that we did not get cornered by the onion brokers, as had happened to us a while back in Oraimutia with potatoes.

We waited for prices to go up, but it did not happen. We ended up selling our produce in a panic at KShs 35/= per kilogram, not to mention the cost of extended storage; and the cost of harvesting and packaging, which the first set of brokers was ready to cover.

I remember vividly what a neighboring farmer had told me when we were haggling with a buyer who wanted to buy at KShs 55/=. The farmer had said that the best policy was to sell produce at prevailing market prices because a cartel of brokers controlled the market, and it was almost impossible to out-maneuver that cartel.

We still grow onions today because, despite the marketing challenges, the crop guarantees a reasonable return compared to the other cash crops we have tried.

But why do cartels seem to emerge whenever small-scale farmers discover a cash crop that promises to give them a well-deserved and much-awaited break? Perhaps it is time for us to consider joining one of these cartels. After all, as the adage goes, if you cannot beat them, then join them - good food for thought.

CHAPTER 7

Physics 101: Mini-Irrigation Project

*"Success is getting what you want,
happiness is wanting what you get."*
—W.P. Kinsella

IN MATTERS OF INNOVATION, FEW people can beat Muturi, a small-scale farmer in Matathia, whose low-key demeanor is his key attribute. He taught us life lessons in fundamental applied physics. His simple, innovative ideas were unbelievably effective in a mini-irrigation project.

◆◆◆

THE TIME CAME WHEN WE got an almost uncontrollable urge to up-scale production from the Matathia *shamba*. The *shamba* is in an area with excellent climatic conditions for crop cultivation. We had started by growing *dhanias*, then onions. We diversified into other cash crops, mainly spinach and *sukuma wiki*.

The yields were incredible. The main challenge was getting reasonable prices for the crops. We decided to follow the practices of other local farmers and sold our vegetables directly to brokers at the *shamba*.

The value chains for these crops were interesting and different for each crop. For example, in the case of *dhanias*, a broker in Mombasa would buy *dhanias* from farmers through a local agent in Matathia. During the *dhania* harvesting season, the broker would ask the local agent to go around the farms searching for the best quality *dhanias*. When the agent identified a suitable source, the agent would negotiate a price with the farmer. The agent would then communicate the agreed price to the broker in Mombasa. If the broker also agreed to the price, the agent would arrange to harvest, pack, and collect the dhanias from the shamba and deliver them to an aggregation center at Kimende shopping center. The *dhanias* would then be transported by truck to the broker in Mombasa.

The broker in Mombasa would pay the farmer directly via M-Pesa when collecting the *dhanias* from the *shamba*. However, there were instances when the broker would pay for the *dhanias* after delivery in Mombasa. The latter usually happened during the wet season when the produce was abundant. At that time, all farmers were eager to sell their crops and did not mind the broker arm-twisting them to await payment after the *dhanias* had reached Mombasa.

SHAMBA SHENANIGANS

On one particular occasion, Susan and I agreed to sell our *dhanias* to a broker called Lucy for payment after delivery in Mombasa. Lucy received the goods and sent us the first payment of 50%. We never saw the balance of 50%. From that point onwards, her cell phone went dead. We were infuriated by the dishonesty, but upon reflection and considering the small amount involved, we decided to forget about it and move on. It was just one more item in our archive of shenanigans inherent in small-scale farming.

We did not give up. As it is said, there is always a silver lining behind every dark cloud. Indeed, the arm twisting by brokers had taught us a valuable lesson. We needed to completely transform our business model by investing in a water irrigation system. The irrigation system would enable us to have abundant produce when demand was high — in other words, positioning ourselves as the go-to farmers during the dry season. We would effectively dramatically turn the tables on the brokers and their cartels.

We did not want to spend much money on this venture because the *shamba* was small. Accordingly, we did not hire a geologist, a professional engineer, or a contractor. We were confident that our fundamental knowledge of high school physics was good enough for the venture. We contracted Kangethe, the "carpenter-cum-charcoal burner-cum cash crops expert-cum-plumber" for the execution of the water irrigation project.

Working jointly with Kangethe, we surveyed the land and determined that our irrigation system would have four main components. Firstly, a water reservoir located strategically within the *shamba* to facilitate the smooth distribution of water to as wide an area as possible. The second component was the installation of pipes to collect water from a nearby stream and deliver it into the reservoir. Thirdly, and most importantly, a system of pipes to distribute water from the reservoir to the *shamba*. Finally, water sprinklers attached to the distribution pipes. We did not need to write anything down. The blueprint was clear in our minds.

Kangethe put together a small team of masons and commenced construction of a concrete water reservoir with a capacity of 20,000 liters. He then installed pipes that fed water from a nearby stream into the reservoir.

The stream carries water for nine months of the year. It dries up towards the tail end of the hot, dry season, which was a small disadvantage for us, but we were comfortable living with it during the initial stages of our enterprise.

Kangethe and his team finished building the water reservoir in record time. It looked beautiful. It was more beautiful than the Hoover Dam in the United States of America. It was like a swimming pool in the middle of nowhere. We felt good about it.

Kangethe installed a semi-sophisticated series of plastic pipes for distributing water downstream to irrigate the *shamba*. About 60% of the *shamba* lay downstream, and the system was, therefore, perfect. We installed several sprinklers for spraying water on the crops - an engineering feat of commendable local proportions in Matathia.

When the project was completed, I experienced an almost spiritual feeling. It was the feeling that only inventors get to enjoy when they finish building a prototype of their device. There is no better feeling.

Now we just had to wait for the cement of our "swimming pool" to dry up before we could activate the system. Kangethe was an expert in these matters and told us that the minimum recommended duration for the cement to dry properly was 21 days. We waited anxiously for the 21 days, confident we would ultimately have the upper hand over the exploitative brokers and their cartels. What a nice feeling!

On day 22, we called Kangethe and asked him to open the inlet gate valve so water from the stream could start flowing into the reservoir. He did it. After a few minutes, he called back to say that the water was flowing into the reservoir beautifully.

We did not want to visit the *shamba* just yet. We preferred to assimilate the enjoyment slowly and in moderate portions. Accordingly, we decided to wait a day or two. By that time, the reservoir would be full. We would then officially set the irrigation project alive by opening the outlet gate valve to let the water flow into the network of distribution pipes. We would then enjoy watching the shower sprays as the sprinklers danced in unison, signaling the end of exploitation by the brokers and their cartels.

So, on day 25, Susan and I set out on our journey to the *shamba* to commission our first-ever irrigation project. A project designed using principles of high school physics, physically executed using local labor, and to crown it all, was implemented at rock-bottom cost.

It was one of those unique moments when one was engulfed by strong feelings that an event of historical proportions was about to happen. Susan, as always, packed lunch of the choicest morsels befitting such an occasion.

We arrived at the *shamba* in literally no time. And true, the reservoir was full. However, we noticed that Kangethe and his team had forgotten to build an overflow trap. Because of this omission, the water had filled the reservoir overnight. The water overflow had traveled downstream uncontrollably, destroying crops on its violent path. Kangethe had noticed this earlier that morning and had shut the inflow gate valve to stop the overflow.

The overnight overflow was a small mishap that was not going to spoil our fun. After inspecting the project, we asked Kangethe to open the downstream gate valve so that we could bring our project to life.

When Kangethe opened the gate valve, all those present went into a frenzy. The whole *shamba* turned into a giant water shower. The sprinklers danced in rhythm, producing a certain kind of music that I can still hear in my ears even now. It was some jerking sound. It started with great agitation as the sprinklers wiggled to adjust to the water pressure. The wiggling mutated into sporadic hissing sounds as the water jutted out of the sprinkler nozzles. Some sprinklers were hissing, chugging, and screeching, almost like a steam locomotive. They reminded me of the famous Hugh Masekela's Stimela song (Masekela, 2009), especially where he sings:

SHAMBA SHENANIGANS

> *And when they hear that Choo-choo train...*
> *A jogging and a popping and a smoking and a pushing and a pumping and a firing and a steaming and a chicking and a ... whaaa whaaaa...*

I love this number. At Matathia, we were listening to a similar tune, a music composition of the *shamba* angels. If plants could talk that day, they would have said, "Thank you! Thank you! You have done us proud. We will, in turn, give you a bountiful harvest that will be the envy of all the brokers and cartels of Matathia and other brokers in the whole wide world."

But just as we were beginning to internalize the impressive display, two things happened in quick succession. Firstly, two sprinklers decided with a wicked sense of unanimity to simply stop working. The way an angry five-year-old child pushes away a dish of food for no apparent reason and says with intense discourtesy: "Mum, I will not eat this horrible food. I want chips".

Kangethe rushed towards the offending sprinklers, at top speed, without even a care in the world of how wet he would become by passing through the water shower sprays. The sprinklers were not about to start misbehaving in front of the VIPs. He tried furiously to fix the sprinklers, but they would not budge. With immense irritation, he shouted at the top of his voice that the sprinklers were acting up because they were the weak quality type made in China. We shouted back our agreement and promised to look for better brands after the show.

The second thing that happened was that another sprinkler decided to start jutting out water in only one direction, as if to say, "I am getting dizzy from all this swinging motion." Surely, this could certainly not be another made-in-China phenomenon. No matter where it comes from, a sprinkler is made to swing. But no, not according to Kangethe. Some non-Chinese-made sprinklers had a habit of exhibiting this type of bad behavior too.

Two other sprinklers near where we were standing offered a bit of respite. They danced ecstatically and in a rhythmic fashion — a unique kind of rhythm. I listened carefully and could not believe it. I recognized the sound right away. It was funk — a James Brown classic. One of the sprinklers was saying, *gerapa*!, and the other was responding, *geronup* (Brown, 2014). They would do this two or three times, and as if to imitate James Brown, they would suddenly change the rhythm and start swinging *hovyo-hovyo* in a strange zig-zag motion. But this was good enough for the début performance.

As if the mischievous antics of some sprinklers were not enough, we noticed some wetness along the path of some of the primary underground distribution pipes. We asked Kangethe to dig up the soil so that we could understand what was going on. When he dug up a few scoops of soil, a jet of water started emanating from the offending underground pipe. We frantically shut down the entire system so that we could figure out exactly what was happening and align on the best way forward. We agreed that Kangethe would inspect the whole network of pipes thoroughly and carry out the necessary repairs.

But all in all, we enjoyed the show, albeit for only a few minutes. Most significantly, we had a clear proof of concept that our rudimentary irrigation system could work. It was just a matter of a few repairs here and some modifications there, after which we would be ready to go. We returned to Nairobi later that day, feeling elated.

◆◆◆

Kangethe and his team continued to carry out the necessary repairs. He would call us from time to time to update us on his progress. The updates were reasonably routine: "I repaired pipes here and there. I bought three new pipes of a bigger diameter. I built a stand for two of the sprinklers." Nothing out of the ordinary.

Then, after two weeks, we received some devastating news. A huge crack had appeared in one corner of the reservoir. In other words, Beelzebub himself had shamelessly decided to interfere with the project. The news came at a time when we could not travel to the *shamba* because of other more pressing commitments in Nairobi. So, we asked Kangethe to shut the inlet gate valve to stop the inflow of water into the reservoir until we had had an opportunity to inspect the project and agreed on the best remedial measures.

The following Saturday, we traveled to Matathia early in the morning to view the project. And it was true. Right there, in front of our naked eyes, was the humongous crack on the corner of the reservoir.

How and why did this happen? The water reservoir had become redundant.

I called my brother Teddy, a lecturer in the engineering department at Egerton University, to seek his professional advice. He told me that his expertise was in electrical control systems, but he would reach out to one of his colleagues who could give the right advice. His colleague, a mechanical engineer, called me shortly after that. He asked me to send him some photographs to give him a better sense of the issue. I sent him the pictures.

He called back almost right away to ask a few clarifying questions. After I finished sharing the information, he said that there were two fundamental defects in the reservoir's design. Firstly, it was rectangular, which was not ideal. It ought to have been cylindrical for a more even distribution of the water pressure on its inner surface. Secondly, and even more seriously, the concrete structure did not have any reinforcement whatsoever. He pointed out that a water volume of 20,000 liters was quite huge—a concrete structure holding such a large quantity of water needed steel reinforcements.

He recommended that if we were to rebuild the structure and retain a rectangular shape, it would make sense to build a partition wall in the middle to minimize the stresses on the walls. In other words, the reservoir would, in effect, need to look like two square cubes placed next to each other. Further, steel reinforcements were essential.

So, out went our ideas from High School Physics 101. The time for real engineering had come.

SHAMBA SHENANIGANS

◆◆◆

The task of rebuilding the reservoir looked quite daunting, but we were not about to quit. We made up our minds to reconstruct the entire structure again, retaining the rectangular shape to leverage the work already done. We built the new structure with renewed vigor, carefully adhering to the guidelines given by the engineer. We contracted a new plumber from Nairobi, Sammy.

Sammy exuded tremendous enthusiasm. He assured us that he knew everything that was needed to make the project a success.

Sammy completed building the new reservoir and reconfiguring the network of pipes in about a month, but at almost double the cost of the original works, thanks to the high price of steel bars.

The cost of one steel bar was equivalent to the income from 10 bags of *dhanias*. That is why farmers at Matathia never got tired of trying out new things, hoping for a new, better outcome. They would try new seed varieties, modern farming techniques, new cash crops, new fertilizers, new pesticides, and new everything. They never gave up. They never retired, either.

When Sammy and his team finished the work, and the new reservoir was ready for commissioning, he did not even wait for us to go there. He did the commissioning himself and sent us a few photos via WhatsApp to showcase the tremendous success of his labor. We were delighted with this development. He was an expensive plumber, but we did not hesitate to send him his dues.

That weekend, after receiving the good news, we traveled to Matathia to inspect the revamped irrigation system. The new reservoir looked superb. However, for some strange reason, the pressure of the water flowing into the sprinklers had decreased significantly. Something had happened during the past few weeks that affected the water pressure. Sammy had not seen the earlier system in operation and could not appreciate our point of view. According to him, the sprinklers were working fine. In any case, to make things even better, he said he would build vent pipes at strategic locations on the downstream system of pipes. He noted that this modification would eliminate any chances of an airlock and help improve the water flow.

The following weekend, while at the *shamba* inspecting the remedial works, a neighboring farmer named Muturi, a very simple-looking man, showed up. He wanted to speak to me privately.

He told me he had been closely watching what we were doing and had a few concerns about the project. He wanted to offer some friendly advice. He said that he believed that despite our great efforts, we were just wasting our time and money. According to him, the gradient of the land would never allow the water to flow at the desired pressure. Further, it would have been more useful to build the reservoir on higher ground on the upper side of the *shamba* to take full advantage of the force of gravity. He talked about the power of gravity with the sophistication of a first-class honors engineering graduate.

He said the only alternative, given that we had already invested heavily in the concrete water reservoir, was to do three things. One: Buy a big plastic water tank and place it on higher ground on the upper side of the *shamba*. Two: Buy a simple water pump to suck water from the reservoir and deliver it into the plastic water tank. Three: Connect the network of pipes in the irrigation system to the plastic water tank. He also recommended that we fabricate stronger sprinklers at the local *jua kali* metal works because the imported ones we had used previously would not withstand the strong force of gravity after re-designing the system.

If there were angels of irrigation, then Muturi was one of them. His advice was like a breath of fresh air. The amazing part was that the information was coming from a simple-looking farmer. One would never have imagined that he had any plumbing, let alone physics or engineering knowledge. I felt a little guilty that we had not contemplated some of the fundamental aspects of physics that he brought to our attention.

I shared the information with Susan, and we quickly decided to implement Muturi's ideas. We worked with Sammy to implement the design recommended by Muturi.

On the day when Muturi's scheme was actualized, Sammy was ecstatic about the outcome. He could not even wait to give us the good news. The water from the plastic tank was flowing at such high pressure that the few imported sprinklers we had retained could not handle it. Only the sprinklers we had fabricated locally, on the advice of Muturi, were working.

Sammy sent us photos via WhatsApp. One showed water jutting out of a hose pipe connected to one of the distribution water pipes and forming a shower almost 15 feet high. This development was immensely encouraging despite a few mishaps of broken pipes, unusable sprinklers, and the like.

Regarding credit for the project's success, things did sometimes get a bit fuzzy. Many people were involved in the project. However, on the whole, we believe that Muturi deserved most of the credit for coming up with the innovative design changes that enabled us to leverage the force of gravity effectively. Because of him, we got a first-hand appreciation of the tremendous power of gravity. What we had learned in high school was just theory.

This venture taught us the importance of being open to new ideas, irrespective of their source. And perhaps more importantly, never underestimate anyone regardless of their status or station in life.

CHAPTER 8

The KPLC Song

*"Some people never go crazy. What
truly horrible lives they must lead."*
— *Charles Bukowski*

THE KENYA POWER & LIGHTING COMPANY (KPLC) is ubiquitous in the daily lives of the majority of Kenyans. But there is nothing that can beat the omnipresent KPLC song. It encapsulates the core of the KPLC ethos. An ethos that is clearly in need of an overhaul going by a few memorable encounters with the institution.

◆◆◆

THERE IS A POPULAR SONG that is very popular at the KPLC. It goes like this:

All our customer service representatives are attending to other customers. Your call will be attended to shortly.
-- Some elevator music--

All our customer service representatives are attending to other customers. Your call will be attended to shortly.
-- Some elevator music--

All our customer service representatives are attending to other customers. Your call will be attended to shortly.
-- Some elevator music--

All our customer service representatives are attending to other customers. Your call will be attended to shortly.

The good news is that you do not need to download this song from iTunes. It is freely available at +254 703 070707. It seems incredible that even the numerals in this phone number have a certain arithmetical rhythm.

The KPLC song reminds me of a popular bubble gum pop song by the famous Jackson 5 (The Jackson 5, 2009) that made many school kids go insane in the 1970s.

SHAMBA SHENANIGANS

The song went like this:

> *A B C, easy as one, two, three*
> *Are simple as do re mi*
> *A B C, one, two, three, baby, you and me, girl*

So, I would recommend the addition of the following stanza in the KPLC song:

> *KPLC, 0703, as easy as one, two, three*
> *Are simple as do re me*
> *Do re me, this is KPLC; all you have is me*

It is a fantastic song, although some may need to acquire the taste for it. I re-discovered it almost by accident after a conversation with Muturi. He talked to me about an innovative way of boosting the water supply for our rudimentary irrigation system at our small *shamba* in Matathia.

Susan and I were determined to take our irrigation project to a whole new level. Our determination was triggered by the high cost of fuel for the water pump that we were using to pump water from a reservoir into a plastic water tank placed on high ground at one end of the *shamba*.

In discussions with Muturi, we concluded that installing electricity and using an electrical pump was the best option. This option necessitated talking to KPLC to inquire about electricity supply to our premises. I re-discovered the KPLC song as I started following up on the electricity supply.

As our thinking on the irrigation project evolved, the innovative Muturi suggested that if we sunk a borehole, we would benefit from accessing freely available underground water during the dry season when the water flow in the nearby stream dwindled. It turned out that the water table was only a few feet deep. We could find ample supplies of water by merely digging a hole 60 feet deep.

A bonus was that we would not even need to hire a mechanized rig to do the drilling. Muturi himself was an expert in manually digging water boreholes, at a minimal cost. All this sounded like solving a giant jigsaw puzzle in just two quick steps.

We immediately commissioned Muturi to undertake an initial, albeit rudimentary, geological survey of the land to identify the most suitable spot to dig a borehole and put together a team to dig the borehole.

The idea was that when Muturi would strike the underground water, we would install an electric pump to extract the water and push it into the existing steel-reinforced concrete reservoir. We would install a second electric pump or even use the same pump to force the water into the plastic water tank, which would then flow into a network of pipes in the *shamba* through gravity for irrigation purposes. It was Engineering 101.

Muturi assembled a team of five people to dig the borehole. Two people to do the actual digging, two people to extract soil from the hole, and one person to dispose of the soil about 10 feet away from the borehole. He was to supervise the whole operation.

SHAMBA SHENANIGANS

We kicked off the project in earnest. Muturi and his team dug a hole 40 feet deep in three weeks. They struck the water, but the quantities were minimal. The team needed to dig another 20 feet to reach the most productive aquifers to ensure an adequate water flow, particularly during the dry season. However, it started raining, and we had to temporarily halt the project for continuation during the next dry season.

The rains had temporarily obviated the purpose for which we were looking for the additional water supply. This situation also meant that we could pursue the electricity supply without haste.

Our acquaintance, Kangethe, had told us that obtaining electricity power supply was a straightforward process. It was just a matter of informing the local Chief, filling in one or two forms, and *voilà*, the KPLC people would be there in a matter of days to install the power. It was as simple as that. Based on this advice, we contracted a local electrician to do electrical wiring in the small wooden house at the *shamba* as we pursued the power supply with KPLC.

We reached out to the local Chief, as recommended by Kangethe. The Chief was very helpful. He was happy that we planned to do something to enhance the local community's quality of life. He told us that he would try his best to link us to the right people at KPLC.

Three or so days later, I received a telephone call from a gentleman who claimed to be from KPLC. He will remain nameless to avoid any embarrassment. Let us just call him Gringo. He told me that he had learned that I wanted electricity installed on my premises. Further, he had called to let me know that he would help me get electricity supply within no time. He asked for the land reference number and other information required by KPLC for account opening purposes. I complied. He said I did not need to physically fill out the KPLC application forms. He would do it for me. How wonderful!

The following day, I received another call from Gringo. He told me that he was still working very hard on my case but needed a little money to cover the transport expenses of the gentleman he intended to send over to survey the site. He asked for KShs 15,000/= (about US$ 150) for this purpose. It did not sound like a solicitation for a bribe. Not at all. His intentions seemed noble, although KShs 15,000/= just for a site visit seemed on the high side by Matathia standards. I negotiated for a reduced sum of KShs 5,000/= and paid him the money via M-Pesa.

I waited patiently for the work to commence. Two days later, Gringo called me to say that KPLC had assessed the cost of the required installation. The total cost would be around KShs 55,000/=. However, Gringo was ready to work with his kind colleagues at KPLC to have the quotation reduced to KShs 35,000/=. Interestingly, this could only happen if I paid him an additional KShs 10,000/= to share with his kind colleagues at KPLC. I did not accede to his request. After all, Kangethe had said that the Chief was in a position to organize for electricity supply under the government's "Last Mile" program, free of charge or at a maximum official KPLC fee of only KShs 15,000/=. Accordingly, I told Gringo that I would think about it. I did not contact him after that.

Gringo was, however, relentless in his pursuit. He had spotted an opening for making some money. Two weeks later, on a Friday afternoon, he called me. He was in high spirits. He told me that I was an exceptionally fortunate person. Why? Because at that very moment, a KPLC truck was heading in the direction of my *shamba* carrying electricity poles.

Further, if I acted wisely and quickly enough, two electricity poles would be dropped at my *shamba* in the next few minutes, in which case he would guarantee the electricity connection in the following week. But there was a catch! I needed to send him KShs 10,000/= right away so that he could prompt his KPLC colleagues to offload two poles near my *shamba*.

It was cunningness at its very best. If there was a contest for mischief, Gringo would have won it hands down on that day. His scheme had all the winning ingredients. It was so imaginative that it was almost guaranteed to elicit the victim's immediate and lucrative response. It was conmanship at a whole new level. If this was happening in Chicago, there is no question that Al Capone would have hired Gringo on the spot. No interviews. No checking of references. Al Capone would have just said. "Give him a pistol. He has all the essential thug qualities. We can teach him jaw-crushing and knee-breaking later." And just like that, Gringo would join the ranks of the most respected organization of crooks in Chicago.

A straightforward lesson of life that I learned as a young boy was that if it sounded too good to be true, it was probably the whitest of lies. So, I respectfully declined Gringo's generous offer. I told him I did not have the money then and would call later. I did not call him.

After about a week, relentless Gringo called me again. He told me he had visited my neighborhood earlier that week, accompanied by his boss. Further, although he had previously suggested that he could help me get a decent quotation from KPLC if I paid a total facilitation fee of only KShs 10,000/=, his boss could not even believe it. According to his boss, peasant farmers in the neighborhood had already parted with 35,000/= each to get an electricity connection. Further, that an official assessment of my installation would come to not less than KShs 120,000/=, but I had an option of simplifying my life once and for all by paying Gringo and his boss KShs 35,000/=. I politely declined the generous offer. I did not hear from him after that.

◆◆◆

One day while riding in an Uber taxi, the driver and I started talking about incidents of corruption in the country. He narrated several horror stories where he had been a victim of corruption. I, in turn, recounted my experiences, including my encounter with Gringo. He told me that my case was very straightforward. All I needed to do was visit the nearest KPLC office and lodge a formal application for electricity supply so the process would flow smoothly. I would get an electricity connection without any unnecessary challenges. This information was excellent advice coming from an unexpected source.

I went to the KPLC office in Limuru a few days later. The first thing that I noticed was several KPLC workers milling around, enjoying the sun, and probably waiting to receive instructions to go to the field to attend to a problem or do something else. The office itself looked rather interesting. Staff workstations were next to the walls, and three visitors' seats were in the middle of the room. It was not obvious who I needed to speak to for guidance. It was life in another small office world altogether.

I approached a bespectacled gentleman who was wearing a white doctor's coat. I inquired from him about the procedure for applying for the electricity supply. He handed me a form and asked me to fill it. I dutifully filled in the form and returned it to him. He placed it in his in-basket. I asked him what the next steps were. He said, "You just wait. *Tutakuita wakati tukienda* site." That was it.

I waited for several days and did not hear anything from KPLC. Two or so months later, I received a call from somebody. It was not clear whether he was an employee of KPLC or their agent. He told me that he was at Kimende shopping center, a small town located a one-hour walk to my *shamba*, or 10 minutes by *Boda Boda* at a fare of KShs 100/= (US$ 1.0).

He asked me to give him directions to my *shamba*. I spent about 5 minutes explaining to him, repeating myself several times. I could tell he knew the place but was pretending not to know it for reasons that were not immediately apparent to me. Finally, he said that he had understood where the *shamba* was but that it was too far away. He said that based on the directions I had given him, he would make up his mind in the next few minutes whether to visit the site. He never showed up.

Several weeks later, I received a quotation from KPLC showing a figure of KShs 155,967/=. The computation of this amount was not evident from the document. However, I could see the invisible markings of Gringo and his boss all over the quotation. I did not take any action on it.

A quote attributed to Walt Disney says that "Forever is a long, long time, and time has a way of changing things" (Disney,2019). I believe there is some truth in these words. Accordingly, I decided to hold off for some time before going back to KPLC at Limuru to follow up on the power installation. I hoped the subsequent encounter would have less aggravation and I would get the power installed in good time ahead of the dry season in 2020 and at a reasonable cost.

I have had several other dispiriting encounters with KPLC. One of these is still playing out as I write. In early January 2019, a close family confidant, Thomas Okanga, a manager of a tea farm at Kwa Sorovea in Limuru, noticed near his farm an electricity pole that had become loose. The pole had started bending under its weight. This bending had, in turn, caused a loosening of the tension of some power lines, causing them to sag and hang dangerously next to some branches of *hakea* trees. These power lines were near the road and posed great danger. Upon noticing this imminent danger, Thomas immediately headed to the KPLC office at Limuru and reported the matter.

Nothing was ever done, despite follow-up phone calls to KPLC. The repeated requests to KPLC fell on deaf ears, but the popular KPLC tune played out at the beginning of almost every phone call.

After some persistence, with no action, Thomas just gave up but cautioned his workers to be extra careful whenever they were near the loosely hanging power lines. If one of the tea lorries that used that road accidentally touched the power lines, the results would most likely be catastrophic.

While on a visit to Limuru in October 2019, I learned from Thomas that the situation had still not been addressed even after nine months since he first reported the problem. He told me some tea pickers had seen KPLC technicians about a week earlier in the neighborhood. The technicians had been on a mission to reconnect electricity supplies for a neighbor who had just cleared an outstanding electricity bill. And when the tea pickers prompted the KPLC technicians about the danger of the dangling power lines, the technicians had just nonchalantly responded that they would return to attend to the problem later. Astounding!

I was quite dismayed when Thomas finished describing the situation to me. I decided to pursue the matter directly with the KPLC Head Office. I thought that the Nairobi—based officials would understand the gravity of the situation and take immediate action. I was mistaken.

Several years ago, a friend of mine told me that in government, parastatal, and other large hierarchical organizations, there was nothing that evoked greater emotion than a "memo." He said that if you were an employee in one of these institutions and your boss told you that he or she would give you a "memo," you would be sure of an unpleasant fate upon receipt of that memo. So, what better instrument to use for lodging a complaint than a "quasi-memo," an email.

Accordingly, I decided to put the complaint in writing to evoke the right kind of emotion and trigger some action. The email exchange with KPLC that ensued was as follows:

> *Saturday 5 October 2019*
> *To KPLC Customer Service Desk*
>
> *Dear Sirs,*
> *There are some power lines that are dangling dangerously near tea plants. They pose a great danger of electrocuting tea pickers.*
> *Kindly assist in having the power lines tightened and raised properly above the ground.*
> *Attached is a diagram showing the location of the power lines.*
> *Regards,*
> *John Mucai*

SHAMBA SHENANIGANS

Wednesday 9 October 2019
From KPLC Customer Service Desk

Good Evening,
Kindly note we're following up your complaint with the engineer in-charge for action on it.
Regards,
Sebastian Odongo. For KPLC Customer care.

Tuesday 22 October 2019
To KPLC Customer Service Desk

SECOND REPORT
Dear Sebastian,
Earlier today, I was astonished to learn that your engineers had NOT attended to the dangling power lines that I reported on 5th October, 2019 (TWO WEEKS AGO).
The inaction is quite frustrating! I sincerely hope next time round I will not be reporting electrocution.
Is there something that can be done to make the engineers do something about this issue?
Your assistance in this matter would be much appreciated.
Regards,
John

SHAMBA SHENANIGANS

Monday 4 November 2019
To KPLC Customer Service Desk

THIRD REPORT
Dear Sebastian,
Your engineers had NOT attended to the dangling power lines that I reported on 5th October, 2019 (ONE MONTH AGO). This is quite astonishing.

Wednesday 6 November 2019
From KPLC Customer Service Desk

Dear Sir/Madam,
We acknowledge receipt of your mail and a follow up is being done to ensure the issue is resolved. Please share your direct contacts, account no and complaint ref no for ease of communication.
Regards,
Christine Asoma, For Customer Care Mails

Wednesday 6 November 2019
To KPLC Customer Service Desk

Thank you for your message Christine.
My previous reports on this issue have been via email to KPLC Customer Service Desk. See chain of emails linked to this message. I was not issued with a reference number. Kindly issue me with one, if possible, for future follow-up.

SHAMBA SHENANIGANS

Regards,
John

Wednesday 6 November 2019
From KPLC Customer Service Desk

Delivery has failed to these recipients or groups:
customercare1@kplc.co.ke
The recipient's mailbox is full and can't accept messages now. Please try resending this message later, or contact the recipient directly.

This communication was amazing. I hope we will never hear (God forbid) of an electrocution accident in the tea plantations of Limuru. In the unlikely event of such an unfortunate occurrence, I suspect KPLC will deny responsibility for the catastrophe without even batting an eye-lid. The technicians from Limuru will no doubt visit the site immediately upon learning of the calamity. They will fix the problem in minutes and then return to their base at Limuru to continue enjoying the sunshine. Someone at the KPLC headquarters will scramble to craft a press statement to exonerate the institution and issue other high-sounding corporate platitudes extolling the values of KPLC.

If these two incidents reflect the ethos of KPLC, then that ethos is in dire need of an overhaul. I hope the story in this book will poke the conscience of at least one responsible person at KPLC and prompt them to do the right thing for the benefit of KPLC and the people of Kenya.

CHAPTER 9

The Largest Market for Avocados is China, or is it?

"Life is about accepting the challenges along the way, choosing to keep moving forward, and savouring the journey."
— Roy T. Bennett

THE LARGE-SCALE PRODUCTION OF AVOCADOS is a fairly recent phenomenon in Kenya. It received a massive boost following a discovery around 2018 of a huge potential market in China. A pact signed in April 2019 by His Excellency Uhuru Muigai Kenyatta, President of the Republic of Kenya and Commander in Chief of the Kenya Defense Forces, and His Excellency Mr. Xi Jinping, President of the People's Republic of China, epitomized the importance of this market. However, hardly after the ink from the pact had even dried, bittersweet doubts about the ability of Kenyan avocado farmers to penetrate that market started emerging in the media. What should the Kenyan farmer do? But Susan and I can see some light at the end of the tunnel.

◆◆◆

AFTER TRANSITIONING FROM A CHALLENGING potato venture into dairy farming and small-scale horticulture, stories started trickling into the local media that the avocado business was apparently in vogue in some parts of Central Kenya. We started hearing of small-scale farmers who were doing very well from the export and even local sales of avocado fruits, especially avocados of the Hass variety. We did not want to be left behind by this train heading to the promised land. Starting would be relatively easy. But was this another bandwagon to an unpredictable destination? Only time would tell.

Many people had seen the opening in the avocado business. Accordingly, grafted avocado seedlings were available for sale in tree nurseries that had sprung up in different parts of Nairobi and Central Kenya.

Sometime in 2018, we bought several seedlings from Bwana Kamau's tree nursery near Sagana. His nursery was well maintained and appealing to buyers of tree seedlings.

We planted the avocado seedlings in our *shamba* at Matathia and also at Oraimutia. We adhered strictly to Kamau's planting guidelines to ensure optimum yields when the plants came to fruition in three or so years. The key elements were digging a hole 60 centimeters square and 60 centimeters deep and putting the topsoil aside. Mixing the topsoil with two buckets of manure, removing the plastic wrapping from the seedling; placing the seedling in the hole carefully to avoid damaging its roots; and covering its stem downwards with the topsoil/manure mixture. Discarding the sub-soil to leave sufficient space in the hole for the accumulation of rainwater; finally, watering the newly planted seedling.

We had done an excellent job because, after about six months, the avocado seedlings at Matathia developed beautiful green shoots. The young and healthy avocado trees became a new appealing feature of the small *shamba*.

◆◆◆

However, we had no idea that the appeal would extend to the animal kingdom too. A particular mischievous antelope discovered the avocado trees. The animal would occasionally trespass into the *shamba* when nobody was looking and munch the succulent leaves of the young avocado trees. The most annoying bit was that the antelope moved from tree to tree, nipping only the young succulent leaves and deliberately ignoring the equally nice-looking green undergrowth.

Because of the abundance of the avocado trees, the antelope was eating the shoots *hovyo-hovyo*. There must have been something very delicious or addictive about those young avocado leaves. This pure larceny was perpetrated by the mischievous animal unashamedly and with grandiose impunity over an extended period.

Overcome with annoyance, Rasta, a farmhand, came up with a brilliant innovation: covering the trees on the sides with gunny bags for protection against damage by the antelope. This idea worked well for some time, but the gunny bags were biodegradable and decomposed after about four months, leaving the plants exposed to the voracious antelope.

The situation changed dramatically following the installation of a chain-link fence around the *shamba*. This simple action completely turned the tables on the antelope.

One beautiful day, the antelope came looking for the choice avocado leaves, but its usual entry points into the *shamba* were blocked. However, antelopes are intelligent. After surveying the area, it discovered an opening on one side of the *shamba* that had not yet been fenced off entirely. This discovery was a stroke of luck of the highest order, or was it?

The antelope sauntered into the *shamba* majestically and embarked on its usual munching mission. Its vision was clear – to become the most voracious eater of avocado shoots in Matathia. But this vision was short-lived. The days of the antelope were numbered. It did not realize that Zachariah and Phillip had been monitoring its behavior for several days and, on this particular day, had spotted it as it stealthily walked towards the avocado trees.

The two gentlemen waited silently for just the right moment. There were no previously recorded cases of unarmed men chasing an antelope on foot and having even the remotest chance of catching the animal. This did not deter the two accomplished hunters. When they saw that the antelope had become somewhat engrossed in the consumption of the delicious shoots, the two men blasted out towards the antelope at full speed.

The antelope, upon sensing danger, ran away at supersonic speed but was quickly brought to an abrupt stop by the almost invisible chain link fence. The animal collapsed momentarily. Zachariah and Phillip captured it on the spot a few seconds later.

That day, there was a big barbecue at the *shamba*. We learned from Zachariah that the meat was delicious. The excellent taste of the meat was hardly surprising, given that it contained the tasty natural flavoring from the shoots of young avocado trees that the antelope had been consuming for some time.

This event brought some calm to the *shamba*. There were no more strategy sessions to figure out the different alternatives of capturing the antelope or dissuading it from trespassing into the *shamba* and wantonly destroying the young avocado trees.

That said, our interest in avocado farming meant that our ears were super sensitive to any news regarding avocados. In April 2019, we learned that during an official visit to China, President Uhuru Kenyatta had signed a deal with the government of China for the exportation of Kenyan avocados into the enormous Chinese market. We were elated and were confident that we would make a small fortune when our first avocado harvest was ready in three or so years. This was a case of simple arithmetic.

There are about 1.5 billion people in China. Even if one works with a conservative assumption that 10% of these people consume avocados, you are talking about 150 million consumers of avocados, more than three times the Kenyan population. There was no way Kenyan farmers could even scratch the surface in fulfilling demand from all these potential Chinese consumers. Therefore, every avocado farmer in Kenya was destined to become a millionaire. Plain and simple. But why is Beelzebub always lurking out there, waiting to spoil the party for Kenya's honest and hard-working farmers?

In June 2019, Peter Munya, the Minister for Trade and Industrialization, said the following:

> *Usually when you want to export something outside, there are standards you have to meet and when they came to assess the situation of avocados, there were found to be some flies, which made it difficult for us to be allowed to export raw avocados, and a decision was made to have frozen avocados exported.*
>
> *We are looking at building capacity for Kenya National Trading Cooperation to support small-scale farmers to aggregate and that's already in the budget. We have resources to support KNTC to*

> upgrade its warehouses and then export (Alternative Africa, 2019).

This press report was a primer for the even more unpleasant news that was yet to come.

Before venturing into avocados, our research had shown that the best avocado variety for the export market was Hass. We visited the largest buyer of avocados in Kenya at the time, Kakuzi Limited, in Thika, and they confirmed that that was indeed the case. That was the variety that they were buying from small-scale farmers.

Getting Hass seedlings was easy. It was available in many tree nurseries in Central Kenya, including the large tree nursery at JKUAT Enterprises, an affiliate of Jomo Kenyatta University of Agriculture and Technology.

Susan had been supplying fresh vegetables to her friends at the Irene Hair Saloon at Westlands in Nairobi. And as a gesture of appreciation, the ladies who ran this beauty shop always kept for Susan any newspaper articles they came across relating to agribusiness. The articles included the pull-out magazines on agriculture available in the Saturday Nation and Saturday Standard newspapers, entitled "Seeds of Gold" and "Smart Harvest," respectively.

The heading of one of the articles in the Smart Harvest magazine of October 19, 2019, read as follows: "Forget Hass, there is a new avocado in town (Mbakaya, 2019)." Good heavens! We had already placed all our bets on Hass, and a Hass tree takes about three years to grow from a seedling to a mature tree bearing fruit, and yet here was someone saying that there was something better than Hass.

The article claimed that there was a new avocado variety called Gem, named after a University of California researcher who had developed it. Further, Gem was superior to Hass. It tasted better, produced fruits throughout the year, and its dwarf characteristics made harvesting easier. The Gem variety was relatively easier to prune, could be planted at a density of 220 trees per acre compared to 120 for Hass, and tended to grow fruits in its inner branches, thereby protecting them from the elements resulting in better yields. Gem trees produced fruits of relatively uniform size and grew faster from seedling to mature fruit-bearing trees (Mbakaya, 2019).

This information was not the kind of news that would uplift the souls of the many farmers who had already invested in Hass avocados. And as if this was not painful enough, in the commodities section of the Business Daily newspaper of October 24, 2019, a huge headline read, "Only 1 in 100 firms meets China rules for avocado export" (Andae, 2019). The story read as follows:

> *Only one firm out of over 100 has met the requirements laid down by the Chinese for export of avocados to the Asian country, six months after Nairobi and Beijing signed the deal.*
>
> *The deal agreed in April this year between President Uhuru Kenyatta and his Chinese*

> *counterpart Xi Jinping allowed Kenya to export frozen avocado to tame pests common with Kenyan fruits.*
>
> *Local firms*
> *The Government, through the Ministry of Trade, has started negotiations to have the directive eased and allow local firms to export fresh avocado as they work towards laying necessary infrastructure to meet the requirements.*

We do not read newspapers anymore. They are instruments used by merchants of doom and gloom to annoy hard-working small-scale farmers. We will hang onto our avocados, come what may.

The Chinese must eat our avocados. They undertook to eat them in large quantities when they signed a contract with President Uhuru Kenyatta. We will not accept any hide-and-seek games. If they do not buy our avocados, we should not buy their shoes, noodles, or trinkets. We should also stop repaying their gazillion Yuan loans. What will Kenyan farmers do with all those avocados?

Despite these challenges, there is hope. Avocados are nutritious. We need to find a way of convincing as many Kenyans as possible to include them in their daily diet. That way, we will not have to worry about exporting our avocados to China.

CHAPTER 10

The Land Where Monday Never Comes

> *"When you stop expecting people to be perfect, you can like them for who they are."*
> — Donald Miller

MALINDI IS A BEAUTIFUL PLACE that prides itself on having many unique attributes. But through two interesting events, an additional hidden dimension was exposed that can only be fully understood through total immersion in the culture of the people there.

◆◆◆

MALINDI IS LOCATED ON THE southeastern coast of Kenya. The famous sites within or near Malindi town include the Marine National Park, the Gede Ruins, and the Arabuko-Sokoke Forest Reserve. The Forest Reserve is a real environmental gem, thanks to the efforts of the Kenya Forest Service.

The coastal strip of Malindi is dotted with world-class hotels and resorts. Also, Watamu's incredibly beautiful snow-white beaches are just a 30-minute drive south of Malindi town.

I first visited Malindi in 1980 while on a trip to Lamu, another unique coastal town in Kenya. The beauty I saw in Malindi while on that short trip remained deeply etched in my memory.

There was only one small thing that nearly ruined my experience. I stayed overnight in a small hotel near the main bus terminus. The mosquito net in my room was a bit old and had a few holes. Because of that, I spent the whole night in a battle with mosquitoes, using the previous day's newspaper as my weapon of choice. How the mosquitoes found the few holes in the mosquito net remains a big puzzle to me to this day. But the nocturnal battle with small insects was not enough to alter my enjoyment of the beauty of Malindi.

The population explosion in recent years, coupled with a shortage of resources, has resulted in a gradual degradation of the town. However, the true essence of authentic Malindi culture is still evident. But clearly, the local government's work to restore the town to its former glory is well cut out.

The town remains a popular tourist destination, especially for the Italians. Their love of Malindi is perhaps best manifested by the many cottages and villas they own dotted around the outskirts of the town. These cottages and villas belong to those Italians who were entrapped by the beautiful panoramic view of the Indian Ocean and the excellent warm climatic conditions and decided to make Malindi their second home. These Italians have integrated well with the local community. It is not unusual to hear a local person speaking to an Italian in fluent Italian or an Italian speaking to a local person in Kiswahili.

◆◆◆

If you stay in Malindi for a while and engage with the local community, you will quickly discover another unique attribute of the place, namely, that it is a land where **Monday** never comes. I learned this through two experiences in 2019—the first involved curtains.

While on a brief visit there, I noticed that many people used a beautiful local fabric for curtains, cushions, and seat covers. Any item adorned in this fabric projected an absolute authenticity of Malindi that I found immensely appealing. Accordingly, I started looking for a local tailor to make some curtains for me using the fabric.

Agnes, a family acquaintance there, introduced me to a tailor called Suleiman. Agnes was full of praise for Suleiman's craftsmanship. However, she forgot to mention his potential for craftiness. I would discover this unpleasant detail several weeks later.

Suleiman talked smoothly and in such refined Kiswahili that he completely won my confidence. I commissioned him to do the job. I paid him the full amount in advance as an inducement for him to do a good job and to do it quickly as I was returning to Nairobi in a few days. He assured me he was the best curtains tailor in town and would deliver my curtains the following **Monday**.

Monday came, but there was no sight of the curtains. I was not overly concerned about this. After all, it was "return to school" time, and Suleiman probably had pending orders for making school uniforms. There was no urgency in the matter. I could wait a little longer.

I returned to Nairobi shortly after that without having received the curtains. After two months of waiting, I asked Agnes to check with Suleiman on the status of the curtains. I was confident that this time around, the curtains would be ready. She called back later, saying that Suleiman was genuinely sorry for the delay and that he had promised to finish making the curtains the following **Monday**. I said okay, "*Sawa Sawa*"!

Three weeks later, a few pieces were delivered on a Tuesday after pushing a little harder and raising my voice one or two decibels higher in conversations with Bwana Suleiman himself. I was happy that, at long last, Suleiman had seen the good sense of fulfilling his side of our contract. After this partial delivery, he said that *inshalla*, he would deliver the remaining pieces "next **Monday**." Next **Monday** came and went. Another **Monday** came and went. Even as I write, "next **Monday**" has never reached.

At some point, Agnes was so infuriated by Suleiman that she threatened to report him to the local Chief. I told her to hold her horses for a while. However, because she was the one who had introduced Suleiman to me in the first place, she felt duty-bound to follow up with him vigorously. So, she continued pursuing him. Eventually, Suleiman revealed that he had used the advance payment for other purposes. He promised to refund the money relating to the portion of the curtains that he had not made. The refund was to be in three equal monthly installments.

The first month-end came, but the refund did not happen. The second month-end came, and the refund still did not come either. And so on, until I ultimately gave up. I commissioned another tailor who did the job in a week. I was happy. He delivered the curtains on a Wednesday.

Suleiman was an old *mzee*. I did not want to harbor any grudge against him, but I just wished he could add **Monday** to his calendar. **Monday** is **Monday**.

◆◆◆

I was ready to forgive Suleiman as an outlier, as far as matters curtain-making were concerned, until I realized that the Suleiman saga was just a primer for yet another episode of elusive Malindi **Monday**s. This time around, the main character would be one Bwana Rashid, a carpenter, and the saga would revolve around furniture.

Authentic handmade Malindi furniture should fall into the category of classic works of art. The furniture can be highly appealing if made well by a good carpenter. It adds tremendous value to any space where it is placed.

While on another brief visit to Malindi, I decided to obtain a few pieces of hand-made furniture, two small tables, and some kitchen furniture. I searched for a good carpenter without much luck until Agnes found a solution. She recommended a gentleman called Bwana Rashid. She vouched for his craftsmanship but didn't know about his enormous world-class skills in craftiness.

I commissioned Rashid to make the furniture. And since I had learned my lesson the hard way, I avoided paying for the furniture in advance. I paid Rashid only one-third of the money. We agreed that I would pay the balance upon delivery of the complete set of furniture. Once again, I was told that the furniture would be ready "next **Monday**."

A few pieces of the furniture were delivered in drips and drubs. And the story was the same as in the Suleiman case. "*Mzee, utapata hiyo nyingine* **Monday**" (You will get the other items on **Monday**). What was it about **Monday**s in Malindi?

Bwana Rashid asked for additional money, but I stuck to my guns. I knew all the tricks of Malindi craftsmen. I insisted that I had to see the complete set of furniture before I could part with even one more cent. My earlier lessons with Suleiman were enough.

Around week 8, by which time I had returned to Nairobi, Agnes told me that Rashid had delivered the two small coffee tables that I had ordered. Further, Rashid had indicated that the fabrication of the remaining pieces was in progress.

Bwana Rashid himself called me a little later to confirm that everything was now on the roll and that all the remaining furniture would be ready by "next **Monday**," but on one condition. He needed some money to buy the timber that was essential for making the remaining pieces. He spoke so convincingly that I did not think there was even an iota of craftiness involved. I loosened my guard and sent him another one-third of the money via M-Pesa. That was the last communication that I would have with him.

He went into hiding. Agnes tried tracking him down, but he was nowhere to be seen. Bwana Rashid had suddenly vanished into thin air. Just like that!

When I was growing up as a small boy in Nakuru, there was a story doing the rounds that the coast was the land of apparitions. The most popular version of it was that beautiful Swahili women would suddenly change into cats. So, when Agnes informed me that she had gone looking for Bwana Rashid in his workshop multiple times and could not find him, I wondered whether Rashid was one of those who could turn into a cat on a whim.

Three weeks later, Agnes gave up the search for the elusive Bwana Rashid. And as in the Suleiman case, I commissioned another carpenter to finish the job. He said he would finish the job on a Friday, and I breathed a sigh of relief. The carpenter did not realize it, but the mere mention of Friday meant a lot to me.

CHAPTER 11

You can get Chapatis at the Lands Office

> *"It's really a wonder that I haven't dropped all my ideals, because they seem so absurd and impossible to carry out. Yet I keep them, because in spite of everything, I still believe that people are really good at heart."*
> — Anne Frank

THE ROLE OF THE MINISTRY of Lands in Kenya is so important that every Kenyan is destined to make a pilgrimage to the Ministry at least once in their lifetime. It is not a wonder that a typical day there is like a market day, perhaps a symptom that the Ministry is overwhelmed with pilgrims from all over the country. The good news is that there is visible evidence of improvements in service delivery, including digitization of searches of property records.

♦♦♦

MINISTRY OF LANDS IN KENYA DESERVES some praise for making huge leaps in improving customer service in recent years. The Ministry has transformed into a professionally run organization, a far cry from the apparent dysfunction of yesteryears. However, there is still much room for improvement, as I came to learn in June 2019.

One of the most notable accomplishments was the digitization of searches for property titles. The digitization initiative was a great program that was intended to benefit many Kenyans. Rather than wasting their precious time going to the Lands Office to search for property records, a Kenyan can accomplish the same purpose in the luxury of their home, office, or cyber cafe. Things could not get better than that.

However, in June 2019, I realized that digitization had a special meaning at the Ministry. But perhaps that June was predestined as my time for a pilgrimage for shenanigans at the Ministry.

On **Monday**, June 10th, I submitted an online search of a property. I received a digital response from the Ministry saying:

> *HI, PLEASE AVAIL THE ORIGINAL TITLE AT THE CENTRAL REGISTRY, NAIROBI, FOR UPDATING.*

SHAMBA SHENANIGANS

The "hi" followed by the "please" were exceptionally pleasant. This salutation was the most reassuring I had ever received from a government office. I was used to the more common and mundane address, "Dear Sir," followed by something like:

> *Ref: Your Letter Bla Bla Bla*
>
> *If you do not do X within 30 days from the date hereof, thence you will either be smacked, frog-matched, or flogged, in public, or all three, at 12:00 noon instant on Tuesday 2 June as time is of the essence in exercise of the powers conferred by Section 13 of the Smacking Act (1902) thereof and the accompanying Statutory Orders, and per the Respectful Treatment of Offenders Rules and Regulations (Special Gazette Notice No. 2 of 1903) heretofore referred to as the RTO Regulations; of which you will be required to pay all the attendant costs as well as disturbance allowances of the smacker, frog-match master, and or the flogger, or any other costs that may accrue consequent on the said public duty of all the officers involved without prejudice and subject to the due sanction of the Minister-in-charge.*
>
> *Finally, be warned that this is not a joking matter, so do not even dare to contemplate or entertain any thoughts of unwarranted clemency to the contrary or otherwise. If in doubt, feel very free to*

contact the undersigned for the necessary clarifications at the usual fee a receipt of which will be duly provided upon express request in writing properly authenticated by two adults of 80 years and above as failure to do so will be deemed to be your irrevocable acknowledgment that you fully understand the consequences of the infractions set out above.

Remember that anything that you say will be held against you.

Your most faithful servant,
Kaa Chonjo, AVGG (K)
A Very Good Gentleman

So, the "hi, please" from the Ministry of Lands sounded like the salutation of an angel. The accompanying message was a gracious invitation for me to make my 2019 pilgrimage to the Ministry.

On Thursday, June 13th, I embarked on my journey to the Ministry, at Ardhi House, in Nairobi, adorned in a gray suit and matching tie, the kind of dress code that occasionally evokes some respect in some places such as the Ministry. Everything counts in these matters.

When I arrived at the Ministry, I was immediately struck by the excellent organization of the place, right from the security entry gate. The security check was very decent —

none of the rough frisking that happens at some airports. The security officer then asked me to proceed to another security office located about 20 meters away from the main gate. I was handed a green-colored badge at the security office in exchange for my ID. The ID would be returned to me in exchange for the badge after completing my mission in the Ministry. When I explained the purpose of my mission, a National Youth Service attendant courteously asked me to proceed to the Banking Hall, located about 30 meters from the security office.

When I entered the Banking Hall, I was pleased to see a nice-looking reception counter manned by three charming officials. Once again, I explained the purpose of my mission, and one of the officials politely asked me to proceed to Counter Number 6.

Counter Number 6 was another world altogether. I joined a somewhat disorderly queue and waited for my turn to be served.

The line moved painfully slowly, with intermittent disruptions by some newcomers who seemed to have a bloated sense of self-importance. These individuals believed they deserved to be at the front of the queue. This attitude enraged those already on the line.

Why would the Ministry not just issue visitors with numbered slips to facilitate an orderly first-come-first-served service routine like most banks nowadays, I wondered? Issuing such slips would be a simple process innovation that would eliminate the apparent disorder at counter Number 6 and a few other counters.

In any event, after the intermittent annoyances, I eventually reached the front of the queue. I was pleased to meet face-to-face with one of the busiest human beings on earth. I handed him the self-explanatory note I had received digitally from the Ministry. I gave him the original title deed too. He perused the documents and asked me to step aside briefly and wait for feedback. This reaction was a little irritating, given the amount of time I had spent in the queue. However, I reasoned that there had to be a good reason for the gentleman asking me to step aside and wait for feedback. I decided to take it easy.

I waited, waited, and waited, occasionally making direct eye contact with the busy official to ensure he did not forget me. Thirty minutes elapsed, one hour passed, and I still did not receive any feedback.

Under different circumstances, it would have made sense to leave and return on another day for the feedback. Unfortunately, I had handed the official the original title deed without a written acknowledgment, and horror stories of a supermassive black hole in the Ministry into which documents tended to disappear were still fresh in my mind. Because of this, I could not leave the Banking Hall even for a brief moment. After waiting for an hour, I started feeling that the feedback I was waiting for was imminent. My periodic glances at the busy official did not seem to have any effect on him. Indeed, at some point, my attention was drawn to other activities that were happening in the Banking Hall.

A few counters seemed to have a ceaseless beehive of activity as the service seekers handed in different types of papers with all sorts of official-looking markings on the documents. This action was followed by an almost mechanical response by the Ministry official at the counter. He or she would skillfully peruse the papers, ask clarifying questions, and then hand back the documents to the service seeker for some further action; alternatively, retain the documents for further processing by other Ministry officials in the back office. I continued waiting, waiting, and waiting! I was standing all this time because there were no free seats in the Banking Hall.

At another moment, my attention was drawn by the unusually large number of women present, just like in a market. The women had taken most of the visitors' seats in the Banking Hall. Many other people, adorned in blank empty faces, were standing idly at different spots in the Banking Hall. Others were fidgeting on their cell phones, while others were drowsing with their eyes, sometimes half-closed and sometimes half-open. All these crowds of people were waiting for something.

Other people were moving around casually, having the occasional small talk with their acquaintances. The one common feature across the entire Banking Hall was the buzzing sound of people talking and producing noise at different decibel levels. Upon close observation, I noticed a pleasant carnival-like atmosphere that was gradually developing, epitomized by the jovial behavior of one woman. She was moving around the Banking Hall like a safari ant. She seemed to be a friend of everyone. She would "high five" one person, talk in jest with another, and so on. She appeared to be a celebrity of some sort, perhaps a "title deed conveyancing queen," or so I thought. It struck me that she was the luckiest soul in the gathering of humanity in that Banking Hall at that time. The world would be a much better place if there were more people like the "title deed conveyancing queen."

When lunchtime approached, I saw another lady walk in carrying a big bag. She passed near where I was standing. I could not prevent my eyes from peeping into the slightly open, unusual-looking bag. And wonder of wonders! Right there, inside that bag, were *chapatis* upon *chapatis*. It seemed to contain other types of foodstuffs too.

The *chapati* lady moved nonchalantly within the crowded Banking Hall, handing out a *chapati* here and a *chapati* there to people, mainly women, who were seemingly well-known to her. It was not difficult to put two and two together and conclude that the recipients of the *chapatis* were her loyal customers. They had either paid for the *chapatis* in advance or would pay for them afterward.

I also came to a second conclusion. Perhaps the increasing celebratory atmosphere in the Banking Hall that I had witnessed was triggered by tacit knowledge amongst an invisible network of people there that the *chapati* lady was just about to make her lunchtime entry into the Banking Hall.

However, the buzzing sounds of people talking in different languages did not subside after the lunch break. The buzzing sounds meant that there had to be something else about this place that I could still not put my finger on. Then, in another sudden stroke of almost wild imagination, I reasoned that the Ministry was probably a special kind of market. A market for sellers of form-filling services and a significantly large number of buyers of these services. This market was bound to emerge almost naturally in this heavily manual form-driven environment. If indeed it existed, as I strongly suspected, this dynamic market would probably remain in existence until such time that the Ministry went genuinely digital.

At 4:00 pm, after waiting patiently for six hours, the officer at Counter 6 signaled me to see him. He handed the title deed back to me and asked me to return the document to him on **Monday** the following week. The document had not been attended to because the person responsible was not in the office that day. He would be back the following **Monday**.

At that particular juncture, I ought to have shouted some obscenities at the official and accompanied it with a loud bang of my fist on the counter to express my displeasure so that everyone in the Banking Hall could hear. However, this type of behavior could be counter-productive while on a pilgrimage in the Ministry. I reasoned that there had to be another approach that could work better.

I left the Ministry feeling frustrated. I was ready to consider my unpleasant experience as a once-off case of bad luck, going by the other positive things I saw in the Ministry. For example, the pleasant service attendants from the Kenya National Youth Service and the re-modeled Banking Hall that gave it a modern look and was a friendly environment for visitors. The areas outside the Ministry's offices were also well-maintained and looked neat.

Later in the evening, I wrote a letter to The Head of the Land Registration Department, Ministry of Lands and Physical Planning, explaining the situation and expressing my frustration. I sent the message via email. I felt this was a much quicker and more effective way to vent my frustration. I hoped that it would elicit a positive reaction.

I returned to the Ministry on **Monday** the following week, as I had been instructed by the official at Counter 6, looking forward to a better experience. I had not received a response to my letter, but this time around, I received exceptional service. So, perhaps the myth that letters and memos enjoy a certain level of importance in government circles may have an element of truth. I completed my pilgrimage to the Ministry with my self-esteem fully restored.

CHAPTER 12

Second Tale of Urban Mischief

> *"The truth is, unless you let go, unless you forgive yourself, unless you forgive the situation, unless you realize that the situation is over, you cannot move forward."*
> — Steve Maraboli

DECEPTION IS A TERRIBLE THING. No matter how cleverly it is contrived, the victim almost always gets to know about it. The Buddha once said, "Three things cannot be long hidden: the sun, the moon, and the truth" (Buddha Quotes, n.d.). The story in this chapter is the second one in this book about deceit. This particular one relates to a relatively more complex scheme. The unique feature of the tale is that it has still not ended. It is narrated as a monster tale because it is similar to the tales our aunties and grandmothers told us when we were kids. The story relates to a phenomenon that is common in Kenya nowadays. Accordingly, the account is likely to resonate with many people. The overall spirit of the narrative is that if you cannot beat them, at least poke some fun at them.

◆◆◆

AS YOU READ THE TRUE monster tale that follows, picture yourself in a small comfortable hut, in the company of other children, around a fireplace, listening to grandma. There is some smoke from the burning firewood in the cooking fire, but you are used to it. In any case, the sheer trepidation of the monster tale you are about to hear from grandma is enough to block out any other sensations that may be triggered by anything else around you.

> *Once upon a time, in the 2000s, all manner of monsters lived in the concrete jungle of Nairobi. There were small monsters that lived in the back streets of Kirinyaga Road. There were also some gigantic monsters. These lived in impressive quarters and swallowed up everything that came their way.*
>
> *The government of the day was angry about the constant misbehavior of the monsters, but there was little that it could do about it. Pursuing justice in an open court system became as elusive as*

chasing the rainbow. At one time, even the Super Judge of the monsters himself had felt utterly helpless and, in a fit of rage, had narrated how he had become a victim of the worst kind of injustice, the like of which had never been witnessed in all jungles. He claimed that certain little monsters in the executive branch of the monsters' government had belittled him. To prove his point, he said that the executive had given each of the two leaders of the duplex jungle legislature the strongest, the fastest, and the most comfortable horses.

In contrast, he, the one and only Super Judge in the jungle, had been demeaned by being given a mere luxury pony. And because individual little monster government operatives had slighted him, he would ensure that dispensation of justice in the jungle would be slow to teach the few monsters in the executive a lesson. In other words, the adage that justice delayed was justice denied would be turned upside down in the jungle courts.

The small and the big monsters were very happy about this state of affairs because they knew they could do all manner of things and get away with it.

SHAMBA SHENANIGANS

The money business in that jungle was big. There were a few wealthy lenders and many borrowers of money.

If a small monster wanted to borrow some money, all they needed to do was reach out to a monster bank. The monster banks were ready to lend money to small monsters but had severe conditions, as you will learn in a minute.

There were many other small lenders too. These small lenders were very friendly. They were popularly known as SACCOs. If a little monster wanted to borrow from them, all they needed to do was find four other small monsters who would act as guarantors. In other words, the guarantors would undertake to repay the loan to the SACCO in case the borrower monster failed to repay the loan for one reason or another.

Many exciting things happened in the money business. There was one particular transaction that surprised many monsters. Let me first tell you the gist of it so you can follow the details.

A small female monster borrowed some money from one of the SACCOs. She then refused to repay the loan. Because of this, the unlucky guarantors were forced to pay the money she borrowed from the SACCO.

The unfortunate part is that she had enough money to repay the loan, but no amount of persuasion from the guarantors would motivate her to repay the money to the SACCO. In other words, she took advantage of the guarantors – a massive breach of trust that greatly surprised the guarantors.

The guarantors strongly believed that the big monster bank aided the small borrower monster. The big monster bank was only interested in getting the little monster to repay another loan that she had obtained from the big monster bank.

So, children, if you have followed me so far, you will be able to understand the intricate details of exactly how that saga unfolded.
Are you ready?

Yes

In that big jungle of Nairobi, there lived a lady called Sungura Mjanja. She seemed humble and exuded great politeness. But the wise ones later came to learn that what you saw is not what you got. Beneath that veneer of holiness was a certain subliminal cunningness only found in the jungle.

One day, Sungura Mjanja wanted to borrow some money to start a small jungle business in the Small Monster Eateries (SME) in the bushes on the eastern side of the Nairobi jungle. Sungura Mjanja borrowed some money from a big monster called Behemoth. Behemoth's terms of the loan were simple, "Pay up, or I Eat You up.

You would be in big trouble if you angered Behemoth, for example, by dilly-dallying in remitting your loan installments. Behemoth would mercilessly devour you before you could even utter the first syllables of the famous short sentence "help me," a sentence that was heard quite often in the thick bushes of Kirinyaga Road.

Behemoth fed on a variety of ignorami and had continued to grow bigger and bigger by the day. Indeed, small monsters occasionally saw Behemoth running around in the bushes, in the company of multiple ignorami from all walks of life. The aims of this activity were, firstly, to enable Behemoth to shed some fat. Secondly, to keep the ignorami in good condition for consumption by Behemoth later.

SHAMBA SHENANIGANS

Behemoth's humongous wit and voracious appetite were narrated in whispers in corporate boardrooms of small and medium monsters who aspired to become as big as Behemoth. They would say that Behemoth did not have intestines -- just one big black hole in its stomach. It did not ruminate what it gobbled. If you were unlucky to cross its path, you would be swallowed on the spot and disappear. Just like that! Kaput! Gone! So, you can imagine the risk that Sungura Mjanja was facing.

But Sungura Mjanja was clever. She conjured up a scheme to borrow some more money from a SACCO called Twiga, just in case her SME did not go as planned and she could not repay the loan from Behemoth, the consequences of which would be unimaginable.

The Twiga was famous for lending out money at low-interest rates, as long as the borrower could assemble some guarantors for the loan. This requirement was not a problem for Sungura Mjanja. She had a lot of kind friends. She was able to assemble a team of guarantors who she secretly nicknamed the Ignoramus Quartet. Twiga was satisfied with the undertakings of the Ignoramus Quartet and lent Sungura Mjanja all the money she needed.

SHAMBA SHENANIGANS

Sungura Mjanja assured the Ignoramus Quartet that she would repay Twiga the money in small installments with money coming to her regularly from a fresh, lovely, and progressive patron, the Real One.

Sungura Mjanja vowed before the Ignoramus Quartet that if anything were ever to happen to her relationship with the Real One, she would ask the Real One to send part of the divorce package to Twiga to clear any outstanding loan balance.

Everything went according to plan for several months. Then the unexpected happened. Sungura Mjanja and the Real One parted ways. The Real One paid Sungura Mjanja a big divorce package. Sungura Mjanja was happy but not happy enough because she wanted more.

Meanwhile, as previously agreed with Sungura Mjanja, the Real One deducted a small amount that was supposed to go towards clearing Sungura Mjanja's outstanding loan with Twiga. Unfortunately, the Real One mistakenly sent this money to Behemoth instead of Twiga. And that is where the trouble started.

SHAMBA SHENANIGANS

The Real One realized a mistake had occurred and called Behemoth in a panic and said, "please return the money to me so that I can forward it to the owner, Twiga.

However, Behemoth would not have any of this. As far as Behemoth was concerned, the money belonged to Sungura Mjanja - and Behemoth, by extension, full stop. The Real One, Twiga, and the Ignoramus Quartet could as well jump into the deepest end of the deepest sea.

The jungle judicial system was in a quandary anyway, so there was very little that this jungle trio could do to Behemoth and Sungura Mjanja. So, Sungura Mjanja and Behemoth laughed, laughed, and laughed all the way to the bank. They have never stopped laughing.

The Real One, Twiga, and the Ignoramus Quartet trio never gave up the quest for justice. They were confident that one day they would have the last laugh.

So, children. When you grow up and go into the big urban jungles, be careful of the small mischievous monsters and the big monsters. Some of them can devour you and not even bother to disappear

SHAMBA SHENANIGANS

because of their confidence that no monster will ever discover their horrible acts.

Some aspects of this monster story are still playing out in the urban jungle of Nairobi. Depending upon how that ending unfolds, the final ending may be narrated in another book in the series.

CHAPTER 13

The Tent of Gastronomical Delights

"If you tell the truth, you don't have to remember anything."
—Mark Twain

THERE ARE ONLY FEW OCCASIONS when the Kenya farmer gains the recognition they truly deserve. The morning of May 25, 2018, was unique. The organizers of a conference held in a leafy suburb in Nairobi made sure that all farmers who had come from all parts of the country to attend the conference stood out conspicuously from the rest of the delegates. The farmers, adorned in a badge inscribed with the important title, "FARMER," walked into the conference hall majestically, full of energy and excitement. A whiff of a cataclysmic step change in the potato agribusiness in Kenya was in the air, and thoughts of the attendant gains to the farmers were heart-warming. But little did the farmers know that another hideous ulterior motive motivated the momentary badge-related glory bestowed on them by the conference organizers.

◆◆◆

WHILE ON A REGULAR VISIT to the Irene Beauty Shop at Westlands, Susan was given a copy of the "Smart Harvest" pull-out of the Saturday Standard newspaper. She had received numerous such newspaper pull-outs from her friends at the salon in appreciation for the fresh farm produce she had regularly supplied them. These pull-outs had proved very useful. For example, they contained listings of upcoming agribusiness events that were of interest to farmers.

On this particular occasion, Susan's attention was drawn to an advertisement for the National Potato Conference 2018 at Kenya Agricultural & Livestock Research Organization (KALRO) offices in Nairobi on May 24th and 25th, 2018. Entry to the conference would be free. Potato farmers in Kenya were the target audience, as well as other stakeholders in this sub-sector. Given Susan's history in potato agribusiness, this particular event was of great interest. She resolved to attend.

The venue of the conference was the KALRO premises, within the posh leafy suburb of Loresho, in Nairobi. Susan attended the second day of the meeting.

All delegates were required to register themselves at the main gate into the KALRO complex. They were required to reveal their respective stations in life so that the organizers could give them an appropriate badge.

All farmers needed to be distinguishable from other delegates. Susan presented herself as a proud farmer. Other farmers from Kinangop, Meru, Elgeyo Marakwet, Bomet, and other far-flung places did the same. As they registered, there appeared to be a certain sense of camaraderie amongst the farmers. The tremendous sense of importance bestowed upon them at that very moment, at the main gate, helped solidify friendship amongst the farmers. The big and bold title "FARMER" inscribed on the badge issued to each of them clearly manifested the importance bestowed on the farmers.

Conference organizers asked all delegates to wear the badge at all times when they were within the KALRO premises. This requirement was standard practice in conferences of this type, primarily for security reasons. However, in this particular instance, there was another ulterior motive that would emerge later in the day.

After registration, the farmers walked majestically into the conference hall, gleaming with a newly found sense of pride. At long last, they were getting the kind of recognition they truly deserved, especially given that farming was the mainstay of the Kenyan economy.

Susan learned that on a preceding day, conference organizers exposed farmers to different aspects of the potato value chain. These aspects included the production of potato seeds, irrigation techniques, soil nutrition and storage of potatoes, financing of potato agribusiness, and the regulatory environment.

Plenary sessions were held on the second day, covering different thematic topics, notably policy and regulations in the potato industry, optimizing production to meet global standards, improving efficiencies in potato markets, and spurring innovation in the value chain.

The sessions went well. The presenters remained true to the conference theme, namely, "Enhancing Technologies in Potato Value Chains for Food Security and Agribusiness" (NPCK, 2018).

The speeches, presentations, and discussions were very insightful. For example, the representative from Grow Africa revealed that crop yields had been declining by 11% annually due to various factors. At the same time, Kenya lost approximately 19% of potatoes across the value chain due to poor post-harvest handling. She tabled various suggestions for dealing with these problems, including technological interventions, improvements in storage, and other measures.

The governor of Elgeyo Marakwet vividly described the challenges that the more than 50,000 small-scale potato farmers in his county were facing. The challenges included lack of capital for cold storage, low-quality seed, and fluctuation in market prices. The pricing challenge was familiar to Susan. A surprising and disturbing point mentioned by the governor was the problem of the stunted growth of children in his county. He said this problem was partly attributable to low local consumption of the very produce coming from the farms there. Farmers in the county sold most of the food crops outside the county, including exportation to Tanzania and Uganda.

Perhaps the message that must have sounded like music to the potato farmers at the conference was the announcement by the Permanent Secretary in the Ministry of Agriculture and Irrigation that the government intended to gazette a 50kg potato packaging and pricing policy effective July 1st, 2018. This policy would bring to an end the exploitative practices of potato brokers that were familiar to Susan.

[The new regulations came into effect in April 2019 after publication in the Kenya Gazette - Legal Notice No. 17, The Crops (Irish Potato) Regulations, 2019. The regulations prescribed stiff penalties for the wrongdoers. The National Assembly passed the new rules into law in the first week of May 2019. The new legislation was later launched at KALRO by the Cabinet Secretary for Agriculture end of May 2019.]

Many other valuable things came out of the conference. For Susan, the most important thing was the realization that the government, in partnership with other stakeholders in the sub-sector, was alive to the potato agribusiness realities. Also, the government was taking positive steps to address the situation, particularly the numerous challenges in the small-scale potato farming sector. These insights were invaluable to Susan, as she had been in the thick and thin of that business a few years earlier. Credit for this goes primarily to the National Potato Council of Kenya, which spearheaded the government's agenda in the potato sub-sector.

On this second day, the morning session ended well, with the usual hand-clapping by delegates in appreciation of the various presentations. It would have been a perfect morning session were it not that the conference had started late. Some VIP guests arrived late and sauntered into the meeting in the middle of presentations, disrupting the smooth flow of the agenda. Over-enthusiastic paparazzi exacerbated the disruption. The "clack-clack" of the cameras and the intense light from the video photography team were significant inconveniences. That said, it was a value-added morning for the delegates.

◆◆◆

What followed after the morning session was the most memorable part of the conference for Susan and many other farmers. The moment of truth for the farmers and their immaculate badges had arrived. It was lunchtime.

The master of ceremony (MC) walked onto the stage to make an important announcement. It was time to go for lunch. All delegates wearing a badge marked "FARMER" were asked to proceed to a massive tent in the middle of the KALRO playing fields. The MC said that lunch was waiting for the farmers there.

All the other guests, including government bureaucrats, suppliers, experts, consultants, and other non-farmers, were invited to join the event organizers in a small tent. The tent was just a few feet away from the conference hall, so this group of people sauntered there casually.

As the herd of farmers headed towards their destination, Susan, and the others in that herd, could not help peeping into the small tent. Inside the tent were hot plates containing all manner of mouth-watering delicious dishes. Even the aroma emanating from that small exclusive tent and the general ambiance of the enclosure seemed somewhat of culinary heaven. For once, Susan felt the almost uncontrollable urge to abandon her title of "FARMER" and join the other important people in the small tent.

But the conference organizers were too clever by half. There was no way that anyone was going to remove their badge. If you had declared that you were a farmer at the time of registration, then too bad. You had to remain a farmer throughout the conference. Susan wished that she had registered as an "agricultural consultant." They would have given her a badge befitting that title, guaranteeing her entry into that small tent of gastronomical delights (the TGD).

But there was hope. The TGD was probably a microcosm of life in the huge tent. The magnificence of the TGD was perhaps making the hungry farmers unnecessarily anxious, Susan thought. So, she and the rest of the farmer herd proceeded dutifully like Masai cows into the huge tent.

The lunch that was waiting for them in the big tent was a spectacle to behold. It was a lunch comprised of cold mandazis and a cup of tea or coffee for each farmer.

The conference organizers had, in effect, with a simple sleight of hand, managed to divide and concur. The farmers, who were the majority, were fed on a non-lunch disguised as lunch. Further, the big tent was located strategically in the low-level fields of the KALRO complex, quite a distance from the conference hall, to discourage any temptations of any farmer trooping back to the TGD.

Meanwhile, the other important delegates continued to move into the TGD with kingly casualness - a casualness that reflected their diverse levels of sophistication. These delegates proceeded to enjoy expensive heart-rending cuisine amidst joyous smiles and pretentious small talk typical in these types of gatherings.

One can only imagine what went on in that small tent of gastronomical delights (the TGD):

As the important guests continued streaming into the TGD, the sound of the chit-chat started growing louder as the voices of the guests attempted to compete with the clanking and rattling sound of different types of sophisticated cutlery and crockery as the caterers were putting the finishing touches to the setup of the lunch tables.

The sophisticated cutlery and crockery included knives, steak knives, fish knives, dessert knives, teaspoons, soup spoons, and dessert spoons. That was not all. There were forks with extra-long tines for eating spaghetti and noodles and seafood forks for eating crustaceans. On top of each table were at least four different types of drinking receptacles, such as teacups, coffee mugs, and water glasses. Wine glasses, champagne glasses, and cocktail tumblers were also available. There were multiple types of plates too. They included soup, appetizer, side plates, and, most conspicuous of all, extra-large lunch plates.

The arrangement of the tables was indeed a work of art. Some guests were so mesmerized that they even took photographs of the lunch tables before taking their seats.

The MC interrupted the guests by clicking on a wine glass with a teaspoon several times. It was time for an important announcement to signal the official commencement of the National Potato Conference 2018 feast.

> *"Your excellencies, all members of the potato brotherhood and sisterhood, suppliers, consultants, stakeholders, other distinguished guests, research students, ladies, and gentlemen. All protocols observed. Lunch is served. We have both buffet and a la carte. It is your choice. Enjoy!"*

"Add a little more spinach, please."
"I will have a leg and three wings, please."
"Give me two big breasts and two extra-large thighs."
"It is my pleasure, madam."
"Give me ribs."
"Reduce the potatoes and add more fillet steak."
"Are you not having the Bomet vegetable salad?"
"Please add some more jacket potatoes."
"I will have pepper steak."

"And would you like it rare, medium, or well done?

"Just give me the most common one, and do it well."

"Stefan, can you believe it? The chef says that he imported the potatoes from Kinangop."

"What? I have never been to that part of Ireland. Did they poach them there too?"

"Give me some spring rolls?"

"Me too."

"Me too."

"Me, I will have five of summer ones and two of winter."

"Do you have lost potatoes?"

"Please check in Lost & Found, behind the main gate."

"You should also have seen big Big Angie. She started with desert and helped herself to half the tiramisu pudding on the dessert table."

"The legs are finished."

"Don't worry. I have three legs. We can share."

"I will have the black forest."

"Me too."

"Me too."

"The chef is excellent. How many Michelin stars does he have?"

"None, but he received a Distinguished Conduct Order medal last year."

SHAMBA SHENANIGANS

> *"He has been doing nyama choma and ugali for more than 20 years. He expects to join the Order of the Burning Spear this year."*
>
> *"I need to speak to the chef."*
>
> *"What is the problem, sir?"*
>
> *"I ordered a buffet more than 30 minutes ago. You people have completely ignored me."*
>
> *"Sorry, sir. We did not realize that you wanted a la carte."*
>
> *"Do I have to keep on repeating myself? I did not ask for a cat. I asked for a buffet."*
>
> *"Are you finished with the plates, sir?"*
>
> *"Yes, please correct all the ditches, but reev the grasses alone."*
>
> *"Please bring 200 more chicken wings."*
>
> *"We ran out of all chicken about five minutes ago."*
>
> *"Just rush to the big tent down there, and ask one farmer from Nandi Hills to chase them. He will catch them in less than two minutes."*

And so on, until the melodious decibels of the call for everyone to return into the conference hall soared above the chit-chat that had reached a crescendo in the TGD. Indeed, the loud voices had somehow also triggered an artificial current of air, filled with wonderful aromas that miraculously started heading towards the oncoming herd of farmers.

The innocent farmers, some of whom had traveled long distances to attend the conference, responded to the return to the conference call. They slowly climbed the hilly ground as they headed back towards the conference hall.

Some farmers nearly collapsed when the air currents emanating from the direction of the TGD hit them. The aromas in those air currents conjured up images of meatballs, sausages, garnished potatoes, *nyama choma*, and fried chicken rolling down the well-manicured lawns of KALRO towards them. These imaginations were manifestations of trauma as energy was sucked from their almost empty bellies as they tried to fight back the onslaught of incredible arrays of aroma from the TGD.

The ghostly laughter that rented the air as the mob of chubby-looking delegates started emerging from the TGD did not help. The psychological torture to the farmers was almost unbearable. None of the farmers even wanted to look inside the TGD.

The conference organizers had demeaned the farmers. But like the extremely tolerant and battle-hardened Kenyans that they were, they did not utter even one audible word of revolt. Some murmured almost silently that they did not even eat *maandazis* in their homes. Some of them decided to pack up and leave without attending the afternoon session.

Ironically, the inconsiderate treatment of the farmers was happening in complete disregard of the fact that they were the primary target audience for the conference. They were the producers of potatoes, wheat, and milk; beef, mutton, eggs, green vegetables, fruits; and many other things that had found their way into the hot plates in the TGD. They were the ones who had clapped vigorously to appreciate the conference organizers and the various presenters all morning.

The TGD clique, on the other hand, walked back into the conference hall, looking as bright and energetic as the farmers had looked earlier that morning. Many of those in the TGD fraternity were laughing gaily. Others had toothpicks protruding from their mouths. Others licked their lips from the sumptuous cuisine their incredible hosts had just served them.

The morale of the farmers was at its lowest ebb that afternoon. It was even doubtful whether those who attended the afternoon session paid any attention to what the conference organizers, other bureaucrats, and the other non-farmers were doing or saying.

The professionalism that was on display in the morning session was significantly tainted by one act of indiscretion on the part of the conference organizers when making lunch arrangements.

◆◆◆

When Susan returned home that day and narrated to me her experience, I wondered what had happened to the Kenyan generosity that was a key cultural aspect of almost all communities in Kenya.

According to the Food and Agricultural Organization of the United Nations, agriculture contributes about 26% of the country's GDP and a further 27% through linkages with other sectors of the Kenyan economy (FAO.org. (n.d.). The conference organizers seemed to have forgotten or were not aware of the importance of farmers to the Kenyan economy. The farmers who attended the 2018 potato conference at the KALRO premises in Nairobi's posh leafy suburb of Loresho deserved better treatment. Organizers of future agricultural conferences should treat farmers as real VIPs.

EPILOGUE

SUSAN AND I LEARNED NUMEROUS lessons from each experience narrated in this book. Below is a summary of some of the important ones.

Chapter 1: A Tale of Urban Mischief
1. Beware of excessive friendliness from strangers.
2. Trying to trick a seasoned trickster has the potential of backfiring in a big way.
3. Sometimes it is better to say "no" to a request from someone who may have psychological power over you rather than seeking a seemingly less painful but convoluted way of declining the request.
4. Deceit seems to be hard-wired in the DNA of some individuals. Watch out for these types, and try your best to avoid them.

Chapter 2: Small Gesture, Big Impact
1. If you see someone perform a good deed for society, take the initiative to show your appreciation. Your action may spur even more positive acts.
2. No matter how insignificant they may seem, small positive actions may sometimes make a huge difference in society. Therefore, do not hold back your good intentions.
3. People tend to react well to positive feedback rather than criticism.

4. If you are concerned about something in society, do not just complain. Try your best to do something about it. Your simple action could trigger a societal transformation.

Chapter 3: Drama in the Savanna
1. If you deliberately damage other peoples' property with impunity, the long arm of the law will eventually catch up with you.
2. You need not hire James Bond to catch a villain; your unassuming next-door neighbor may turn out to be the best spy in town.
3. Taking someone to court may not necessarily be the best solution to your grievances. You may achieve a better outcome by forgiving one who confesses and expresses remorse for their offending actions.
4. There is something extremely disheartening about a *mzee* crying. If you see one doing this, you should know that the *mzee* has a genuine problem or is in serious trouble.
5. Pardoning those who have wronged you and who seek your forgiveness is a virtue.

Chapter 4: Challenges of Promising Potato Enterprise
1. Your entrepreneurial spirit is essential, but it is not the only thing that counts in agribusiness. Some basic research on all aspects of the value chain is vital.
2. Never sign a potato sales contract that does not explicitly describe the meaning of "a bag of potatoes."

3. Life is less complicated when you focus on the part of the value chain where you have the greatest strength.
4. Beware of brokers of anything as they may not have your interests at heart.

Chapter 5: Hay and Debris
1. Jumping onto a bandwagon may not be a wise business decision.
2. Little mistakes by people in an organization can have far-reaching consequences for the organization and its customers.
3. Taking responsibility for one's errors and taking the necessary steps to remedy the situation are great virtues.
4. Dairy farming may be a tough business with minimal financial rewards. But if you spend time on a dairy farm, you may discover other things about dairy farming that may have better meaning in your life than just money.

Chapter 6: Charcoal Burning Venture Beats Cash Crops
1. Do not take the counting skills that you learned in kindergarten for granted. They may come in handy at the most unexpected time in your life.
2. If you observe unusually high demand for your products, do a little research to understand the underlying reasons. The results of the research could surprise you.
3. Never underestimate the importance of bookkeeping in a business venture, especially where neighbors, close relatives, and friends are involved.

4. When it comes to farm produce, sometimes it is prudent to accept current market prices.
5. Do not underestimate the power of cartels in agribusiness.
6. The "rockets and feathers" phenomenon typical in the oil industry does not exist in the onion industry. This phenomenon works in reverse in the onions industry.

Chapter 7: Physics 101: Mini-Irrigation Project
1. It is wise to seek the advice of professionals before undertaking a project.
2. Taking shortcuts can sometimes result in delays and unnecessary losses, with the attendant frustrations.
3. Never give up your ambitions. If you keep on trying, you will eventually succeed.
4. If you put genuine effort into an enterprise, you may attract others with better ideas to help you succeed.
5. Be flexible and open to new ideas. The solution to your problems could come from individuals from whom you least expect.
6. Do not ignore anyone irrespective of their status in life. They could be the missing link in the success of your enterprise.

Chapter 8: The KPLC Song
1. We will withhold the lessons from the KPLC story, for now, hoping that the conscience of at least one person at KPLC will be touched to initiate the action necessary to urgently address the danger lurking in the tea plantations of Limuru. And, more importantly, take a

few positive steps toward overhauling the ethos of the organization.

Chapter 9: Largest Market for Avocados is China, or is it?
1. Always remember the adage that says you should not put all your eggs in one basket.
2. Always have a plan "B" in case your trusted promisor reneges on their side of the bargain in a contract.
3. If you hear that everybody in country X loves avocados, then consume that advice with a little pinch of salt, lest you live to wish that you never heard "country X" and "avocados" used in the same sentence.

Chapter 10: The Land Where Monday Never Comes
1. If a craftsman repeatedly tells you that your order will be ready "next **Monday**," remember that "next **Monday**" is the standard vocabulary of crafty craftsmen.
2. Do not believe those who say that people can vanish and turn into cats. Such disappearances are classic magic tricks usually performed by crafty craftsmen when they are unable or unwilling to fulfill orders for items their clients have paid for in advance.

Chapter 11: You can get Chapatis at the Lands Office
1. If you feel disappointed or angry about something, try having fun with it. It could be therapeutic.
2. Do not be overly excited when you hear about digital transformation. Digitization can have several different meanings. Even an email asking you to travel several

miles to collect a document is a form of digital communication.
3. It is good to cut some slack for those who may be overwhelmed by work through no fault of their own.
4. Wherever there is a group of people gathered together, the chances are that there will be one or more invisible networks at play.

Chapter 12: Second Tale of Urban Mischief
1. Be extra cautious when dealing with the soft-spoken and humble-looking types. They could have a hidden talent for deceit.
2. If you cannot beat them, at least poke some fun at them. It could be therapeutic for you.

Chapter 13: The Tent of Gastronomical Delights
1. People may forgive you for the small indignities you subject them to, but they will never forget.
2. Using food as a tool of discrimination is dishonorable and contrary to many African cultures. Generosity is considered virtuous even amongst those who are least endowed with resources.

SELECTED PHOTOGRAPHS

Susan in the Longonot savanna grassland.
Mt Longonot is in the background.

Harvesting and packing of white bulb onions at Matathia.

Mzee Inziani inspecting debris found in hay at Oraimutia.
Eldoret and Dubai are in the background, watching keenly.

Charcoal burning mounds at Matathia.

Susan observing young avocado trees in the onion *shamba*.
The anti-antelope chain link fence is slightly visible in the background.

Muturi, an expert in gravitational force.
An apprentice is keenly following in his footsteps.

Dangling KPLC power lines in the Limuru tea plantations.

SHAMBA SHENANIGANS

Tree-eating goats captured on camera red-handed.

Beautiful shores of Malindi on a **Monday** morning.
Bwana Rashid is invisible in the foreground.

The wonderful Potato Farmer badge of honor.

TRANSLATIONS

Boda Boda: Motorcycle used as public transport

Dhania: Coriander.

Fundi: Universal term that refers to different types of technicians such as plumbers and masons.

Hovyo-hovyo: Colloquial Kiswahili term that means "carelessly."

Inshalla: God willing

Jiko: Charcoal stove

Jua Kali: Means scorching sun but is used to refer to small-scale traders and artisans

Mandazi: Bun

Matatu: Privately owned minibusses; they are the most common form of public transport

M-Pesa: A money transfer system based on the mobile telephone

Muiko: Long wooden spoon

Mzee: Respectful way of saying "old man."

Njora: A sharp double-edged sword. It is the weapon of choice for Longonot herdsmen.

Rungu: A club with a round head. It is a dangerous weapon.

Sawa Sawa: Polite Kiswahili's way of saying, "OK! That is fine."

Shamba: Farm or field. It is common parlance in Kenya, even when people are communicating in English.

Shuka: A bedsheet. Some herdsmen typically use it as a garment.

Sukuma wiki: Kale.

Tutakuita wakati tukienda site: We will call you when we go to the site

Ugali: A thick porridge, which is a typical staple food in Kenya.

We, niurihite?: You have you paid?

REFERENCES

Alternative Africa (June 29, 2019). More Kenyan farmers turn to avocado farming for huge Chinese market. Retrieved from https://alternativeafrica.com/2019/06/29/more-kenyan-farmers-turn-to-avocado-farming-for-huge-chinese-market/

Andae, G. (October 24, 2019). Only 1 in 100 firms meets China rules for avocado export. *Business Daily*. Retrieved from https://www.businessdailyafrica.com/markets/commodities/Only-1-in-100-firms-meets-China-rules-for-avocado/3815530-5323848-py84fv/index.html

Brown, J. (October 27, 2014). *Sex machine* [Video file]. Retrieved from https://www.google.com/search?q=James+Brown+Sex+Machine&rlz=1C1GCEA_enKE810KE810&oq=James+Brown+Sex+Machine&aqs=chrome..69i57.7903j0j8&sourceid=chrome&ie=UTF-8

Buddha Quotes. (n.d.). Retrieved from https://www.brainyquote.com/quotes/buddha_133884.

Coelho, P. (2012). *The Alchemist*. London: HarperCollins Publishers.

Climate-Data.Org. (n.d.). Retrieved from https://en.climate-data.org/africa/kenya/nakuru/naivasha-11126/.

FAO (November 2, 2019. Better utilization of locally available feed. (n.d.). Retrieved from http://www.fao.org/ag/againfo/themes/documents/PUB6/P621.htm.

FAO.org. (n.d.). Kenya at a glance. Retrieved December 30, 2019, from http://www.fao.org/kenya/fao-in-kenya/kenya-at-a-glance/en/.

Farmers Trend (November 17, 2019). Technology farm in Nakuru. Retrieved from https://farmerstrend.co.ke/technology-farm-nakuru-njoro-dairy-cows-live-fast-lane/.

Fields, J., Caparó Antonio Javier, & Doyle, A. C. (2012). *The adventures of Sherlock Holmes*. Edina, MN: Magic Wagon.

Gakuo, J. (2005, May 11). Let's have the trees, Gakuo tells donor. *The Standard*, p. II.

Ghaligai, F., & Pacioli, L. (1521). *Summa de arithmetica*. Firenze.

Girma, Rossiter, Hennemann, & G.r. (1970, January 1). Soils of the Lake Naivasha area, Kenya: summary of the investigations 1997 - 2000 by the Soil Science Division of ITC. Retrieved November 2, 2019, from https://www.narcis.nl/publication/RecordID/oai:ris.utwente.nl:publications/d92f3f51-b33f-4c77-95d7-92434cc31b34.

Karmali, J. (1993). *The beautiful plants of Kenya*. Nairobi: Text Book Centre.

Macharia, W. (2016, May 9). Retrieved from https://farmerstrend.co.ke/technology-farm-nakuru-njoro-dairy-cows-live-fast-lane/

Masekela, H. (October 23, 2009). *Simela* [Video file]. Retrieved from https://www.youtube.com/watch?v=n4Bb7p9gggc

Maslow, A. H. (1943). A theory of human motivation. *Psychological Review*, 50(4), 370–396. DOI: 10.1037/h0054346

Mbakaya, G.(October 19, 2019). Forget hass; there is a new avocado in town. *The Standard, p12*.

NPCK. (June 2018). Retrieved December 3, 2019, from https://npck.org/past-events/.

Parker, L. M. (1989). Medieval Traders As International Change Agents: A Comparison With Twentieth Century International Accounting Firms. *Accounting Historians Journal*, 16(2), 107–118. DOI: 10.2308/0148-4184.16.2.107

Parliament of Kenya Senate Hansard. (November 28, 2019). Retrieved from http://www.parliament.go.ke/sites/default/files/2019-11/Thursday%2C%2028th%20November%2C%202019.pdf

Sally, Paul, & Beth. (2018, November 2). Technology Farm in Nakuru-Njoro, where dairy cows live on the fast lane. Retrieved from https://farmerstrend.co.ke/technology-farm-nakuru-njoro-dairy-cows-live-fast-lane/.

The Jackson 5 (2009, July 20). *ABC Song* [Video file].Retrieved December 30, 2019, from https://www.google.com/search?rlz=1C1GCEA_enKE810KE810&sxsrf=ACYBGNR1-O9XYF9YdSKHgiRu1ERbxFrJgw:1575489565133&ei=HRD0XfjdB4PjgwebtpvIDA&q=jackson+5+abc&oq=Jacson+5+&gs_l=psy-ab.1.2.0i10l10.1755.4648..8026...0.1..0.319.2143.2-8j1......0....1..gws-wiz.......0i71j35i39j0i273j0i131i273j0i67j0j0i131j0i20i263.k2uERjLyltU.

Waiyaki, W. (2005, April 6). Woman's donation to Kangemi. *The Standard*, p. II.

Walt Disney Quote. (n.d.). Retrieved December 5, 2019, from https://www.azquotes.com/quote/411901

BOOKS BY THIS AUTHOR

The Endless Search For More: A Collection Of True Stories On Money Matters

A collection of true stories that revolve around our continuous search for "more." And while this trait is essential for the long-term sustainability of humanity, John Mucai suggests that we must always strive to appropriately calibrate our desires. And more importantly, adopt a problem-solving mindset in our neverending quest for "more."

Historical Snapshots Of The Great: What Can We Learn From Them?

The quality of life that we enjoy today is a function of the many commendable actions done by individuals in different spheres of life. Some of these people came before us many years ago, while others live amongst us. This book explores the lives of some significant historical figures to determine whether they had any common attributes we can emulate.

Seeking The Right Path: A Search For Spiritual Enlightenment

This book is a chronicle of a personal search for spiritual enlightenment. John Mucai starts by finding out what religion means. He then looks at the different religions and zeros on five major ones: Christianity, Islam, Hinduism, and Buddhism. These religions have a combined following comprising about 80% of the world's population. He looks at their beliefs, practices, and sacred texts.

And most importantly, the many complex questions that emerge from the texts. While the book would be of immense interest to theologians, it is not a book on theology. Instead, it is an attempt by the author to seek spiritual enlightenment by sifting through the religious literature freely available to any ordinary citizen of the world. The author's findings illuminate and hopefully give believers and non-believers a new perspective on religion.

Multiple Dilemmas: A Fictional Story Of Multiple Ethical Dilemmas Based On True Historical Events

Multiple Dilemmas is a thriller based on historical events that raise significant ethical questions. The book delves deeply into challenging situations where ethical considerations are paramount, but the right choices are not clearly evident. The twists and turns in the story will keep the reader entranced for several hours.

Ngurario: A Traditional Kikuyu Marriage Experience

Ngurario is a true story of the multiple steps that John and Susan went through to formalize their marriage according to Kikuyu traditions. The book delves deeply into the drama, excitement, and joy they experienced along the way, right up to the final step in the journey, namely, an elaborate and colorful ceremony called ngurario.

Reminiscing On Basics: Fascinating Science And Maths Ideas For Everyone

Some ideas in science and maths are so fascinating, it is a shame that they are inaccessible to many people. This book is an attempt to fill the gap. Perhaps the curiosity triggered by these ideas will put a new intellectual journey into motion for some people, as it has done for the author.

One Day In The Year 3000

Nobody knows what the future holds one thousand years from now. But one can make some wild guesses. This book peeks into that distant future.

Stratagem: Developing A Strategic Mindset

Have you ever attended a strategy meeting and wondered whether everyone in the forum understood what strategy meant? If you have, you are not alone. Interestingly, many such meetings roll on smoothly with impressive outcomes. That phenomenon is the ninth wonder of the world. Some participants probably spend many hours after the meeting engrossed in self-doubt or guilt, depending upon how loudly they spoke during the session. A cold or hot beverage usually works wonders during such moments of self-reflection. If you are one of those who experience self-doubt but usually emerge from strategy discussions with your conscience intact, you must count your blessings. You are a brave survivor. But whatever category you belong to, you have the cure for strategy-fuzziness right at your fingertips. Strategem describes strategy with exceptional lucidity. Well-thought-out strategies are not only essential for business success; they are critical for success in personal life.

Archetypes Of Human Existence: A New Perspective

Out of the more than seven billion people who inhabit the earth, no two are exactly the same. Even tweens have differences. Every individual has been bestowed by nature's unique attributes. And yet, the behavior of human beings can be reduced to a few archetypes. At the heart of the matter, each human being is one entity comprised of a mind and a physical body, a mind that yearns for happiness, and a body that longs for sustenance. And it is the interplay of these two needs that creates the different archetypes of humans. This book explores a few of the archetypes. It discusses how the ideas around archetypes converge to offer a new perspective on fundamental questions that existentialists have been grappling with for ages. The people described in the second chapter of this book are entirely fictitious. Any resemblance of their names to real people is purely coincidental. However, the characters are real and live among us. You may recognize some of them in your local community, your network of friends, or even in other human networks to which you are directly or indirectly connected.

Number One: Nothing Else Seems To Count

In the modern, highly competitive world, doing well in any competition is not enough. Being number one is what counts. This book traces the lives of five colorful individuals. They are winners in their unique ways from the early stages of their lives. We intimately experience the twists and turns that occur as they enter early adulthood and get embroiled in a contest anchored in the pursuit of business success and love. At some point, each character will realize that things can become highly complex, emotionally draining, and even dangerous when love is in the mix. The outcome of their respective pursuits to be "number one" is astounding. Indeed, the way the story ends offers readers tremendous food for thought.

Fun and Grit: Encounters of Farming Hobbyists

The stories in this book are primarily about people-the people of the shamba (small farm). After working for one of the biggest multinational companies and dabbling in a small-scale farming hobby, one of my insights is that every experience, whether pleasant or unpleasant, gives life its flavor.

Indeed, some of the unpleasant experiences add more spice to life. Having a nice laugh about something is the magic trick in many cases. Laughter is undoubtedly the best medicine for the soul.

INDEX

acacia 23, 56
Albert Einstein 1
Anne Frank 123
Anti-Stock Theft Unit . 26, 27, 29, 30
Arabuko-Sokoke Forest Reserve 115
Australia 23, 24
Bomet 145, 151
Bwana Rashid 167
Celsius 22, 70
charcoal..... 63, 64, 65, 66, 67, 69, 70, 71, 77
Charles Bukowski 89
Chege............................. 49
China 81, 82, 105, 109, 110, 112, 113, 161, 171
City Hall 18
Clinton 54
Customer Service . 60, 100, 101, 102, 103
dhania 70, 71, 76
Donald Miller 115
Dubai 164
Eldoret..................... 51, 164
Elgeyo Marakwet .145, 146
Eucalyptus 23

Food and Agriculture Organization 50
Friesian 51
Gakuo 17, 18, 172
GDP 156
Gede Ruins 115
Gem 112
githeri 5
Githunguri 8, 49, 50
grevillea robusta 23
Gringo.. 93, 94, 95, 96, 98
Hass 106, 111, 112
herdsmen... 22, 25, 26, 27, 29, 170
High School Physics 10184
Irene Beauty Shop 144
isukuti........................... 2, 3
itara................................. 5
jacaranda........................17
James Bond 27, 33, 158
JKUAT Enterprises 111
John Gakuo 17, 18
Judy................................. 54
Kakuzi Limited 111
KALRO . 144, 145, 147, 148, 150, 154, 156

Kamau .. 36, 50, 51, 52, 53, 68, 106
Kamuyu Primary School 23, 25
Kangemi 16, 17, 173
Kangethe ... 63, 64, 65, 66, 68, 69, 70, 71, 72, 77, 78, 79, 80, 81, 82, 83, 93, 94
Kari 18
kasuarina........................17
Kenya Agricultural & Livestock Research Organization 144
Kenya Forest Service....116
Kiama.........................10, 13
Kianda College 16
Kimende .8, 66, 68, 76, 97
Kinangop 51, 145, 152
Kirinyaga 24, 134, 138
Kirinyaga Road 7, 134, 138
KPLC 89, 90, 91, 93, 94, 96, 97, 98, 99, 100, 101, 102, 103, 160, 166
Lake Naivasha... 22, 23, 51, 172
Lake Nakuru................ 2, 23
Lamu...............................116
Langalanga........................ 2
Limuru..........................166
Longonot 21, 22, 24, 25, 29, 33, 163, 170
Loresho......................... 144
Luhya 2
maandazis 154
macica 49, 50
Mae West....................... 47

Mahatma Gandhi 15
Malewa........................... 59
Malindi....115, 116, 117, 119, 120, 167
Mandela 54
Maridadi 51, 52, 58
Marigiti 38, 40, 41
Marine National Park ... 115
Mark Twain 143
Masai...................... 51, 149
Matathia . 3, 8, 63, 64, 66, 70, 75, 76, 78, 81, 83, 85, 86, 91, 94, 106, 107, 108, 164, 165
Meru.............................145
Michelle 54
Mombasa 69, 76, 77
Monday... 38, 102, 115, 117, 118, 119, 120, 124, 131, 132, 161, 167
monster . 7, 8, 14, 133, 134, 135, 136, 137, 138, 142
muiko............................... 6
mukima................... 23, 24
mukimo...........................5
Musaka 51, 54
Muthaiga Police Station 18
Muturi .. 75, 86, 87, 88, 91, 92, 166
Mwangi. 25, 27, 28, 29, 33
mzee 31, 32, 33, 119, 158
Mzee Inziani..... 55, 56, 58, 164
Nairobi City Council 17
Nairobi School................ 18
Nandi Flame.................. 18

National Potato Conference 2018... 144, 151
Ndungu 35
njora 28
Njoro 8, 47, 55, 173
Njoroge 8, 9, 12, 13
Nyahururu 35, 36
Nyandarua 37, 39
Ol Kalou Dairy 60
Ol Kalou Dairy Company 60
Old Naivasha Road 22
Oliver Goldsmith 63
onion 164, 165
Oraimutia....35, 39, 40, 41, 43, 44, 45, 48, 50, 58, 63, 72, 106, 164
Peter Munya 110
Phillip 108, 109
potato ... 35, 36, 37, 42, 43, 44, 45, 47, 106, 143, 144, 146, 147, 151, 156, 158
Rashid 119, 120, 121
Robert Frost 21
Roy T. Bennett 105
Ruaraka 18, 49
rungu 28
Ruto 54
Sammy 85, 86, 87, 88
Shabab 3
shamba. 23, 26, 29, 30, 37, 39, 48, 51, 52, 56, 64, 67, 69, 71, 72, 75, 76, 77, 78, 79, 80, 81, 83, 86, 87, 91, 92, 93, 97, 106, 107, 108, 109, 165
Shangi 37
Sherlock Holmes 27, 28, 172
shuka 28
Smart Harvest 111, 144
Steve Maraboli 133
sukuma wiki 76
Suleiman 117, 118, 119, 120, 121
Tanzania 38, 147
Technology Farm ...55, 56, 57, 173
TGD 149, 150, 153, 154, 155
The Standard ...17, 172, 173
Thomas Okanga 98
Town Clerk 17, 18
Uganda 38, 147
Uhuru 54, 105, 109, 112, 113
United Nations 50, 155
University of California 112
W.P. Kinsella 75
Walt Disney 35, 98, 173
Watamu 116
xanthophoea 23
Xi Jinping 105, 113
Zachariah 108, 109

Made in United States
North Haven, CT
03 December 2022